SUNDHARI THEVAR

First Published in April 2023

ISBN: 978-93-5741-638-2

BLUEROSE PUBLISHERS
www.BlueRoseONE.com
info@bluerosepublishers.com
+91 8882 898 898

Cover Design:
Aman Sharma

Typographic Design:
Namrata Saini

Distributed by: BlueRose, Amazon, Flipkart

Introduction

This is a story of a dad who was immensely loved by his daughter and a father who loved his daughter to the moon. He has left this world but keeps sending her signals that he is always with her. It keeps me going. This kind of love that can never be measured and classified by words in the English dictionary. The kind of love which lingers even after the soul departs and waits for the other to join them. I started to write this as I realized in my journey of taking my dad through his cancer diagnosis and treatment I met so many people and realized that this area is such a black hole. It was an experience everyone was going through blindly. It would really help to find out the definitive possibilities of treatments and then go ahead with whatever is required. I have rarely seen doctors who have said that they cannot save him and always go ahead to experiment and then realize after all the pain that the person has gone through that they are now weak and cannot take in any more treatment. Why not do all your multiple visits and then let them decide how they would want to live their further life to the fullest with pride and honour.

A. P. Thevar was not a name. He was an emotion, a legend and beyond anything an absolute human being – My dad

I am so proud to have him as my dad. So strong. So brave. Even in his pain did I rarely see him shedding any tears.

He was a fighter, never giving up till the end. He will wait for me in the place beyond. I am sure of that and I will patiently wait for the time to join him there. I was told that you do not meet your loved ones in case of accidents so I will be careful in whatever I do.

This is thoughts from the mind and nothing polished about it. I have penned down what I felt and what I went through. Initially I included names and places but then decided to amend that as I am sure dad would not have wanted that to happen.

However, I will ensure I reach this book to them so they realize the other side of the emotions too which they rarely did.

I have written how pathetic sometimes our medical system is and how someone's existence is taken for granted and their death even worse.

Please feel free to reach me in case of any more information that you might need that can help with you or any of your loved ones in their journey of this dreaded disease.

A self – made man who spoke better English than a convent bred me and had a better business acumen than anyone who had a business management degree. I was surprised to see his marksheet post his death when I was going through his records. He had scored just 9 out of 100 in the English language. It did not matter. It showed the kind of effort he put into himself to succeed and to build the empire which he did from scratch. Just being street smart and honest.

With nothing in hand, he had fled from his home in the village at just around 13 years old and got onto a train to Mysore as he had failed his 10th class. He had stolen five paise from his dad's pocket that day and was beaten up. His anger took the greater of him and he decided to run away from home. In the train he met this Christian family who took pity on him and took him under their care. They got him a job in the Indian railways which started off by laying stones on tracks under the hot sun and then went onto becoming a lorry driver carrying loads of material across different states for railway works and finally left as a store manager with a conduct certificate as the best store keeper on records of Indian railways. At that time a known common friend of a friend was looking for a general manager for his Lodge and restaurant in Bangalore and found dad to be extremely smart and well spoken. He was given the opportunity to take up the position and he did. I was being told by his friend that he used to always be impeccably dressed with neatly pressed clothes and clean shoes. He would never step out of the house without his watch and tie and was always punctual. This was extremely important as the guests of this lodge were only foreign guests and people of very highly influential nature. The guests had to be spoken only in English. I remember him saying that Shivaji Ganesan used to stay there as his son Prabhu studied right opposite at the Bishop cotton boys school.

This was a huge lodge and I remember when I was very tiny it had these large stone pillars and was called the "Mashish Lodge". Just next to the lodge was a rundown garage that was not doing well and the owner was planning to give it away . I still don't know what came over dad but he wanted to take that over and then start his own restaurant. It was an extremely brave move as his funds were limited. But he wanted to be his own boss and wanted to run the show by himself.

He was around 28 when he got married to mom and she was barely 16. He used to say that he was not too keen on getting married but went on to it due to the insistence of his elder sister. He did not recollect knowing my mom but my mom had seen him as they were neighbours and was madly in love with him and had told her parents that she wanted to wed only him. So hence they got married. Dad said that he later on went on to fall in love with mom- I don't see how that is not possible as she was beautiful inside and out. I remember mom as a very kind soul, very naïve and innocent and a village clad girl with zero education.

After she passed away at the age of 38 dad told me that as a kid I had told him not to send mom with to my lunch as she could not communicate with my friends in English. I never knew that as I was too small. When I meet her, I have one apology to definitely make

My dad had another younger brother to whom he gave away his railway job when he left. Mom had two brothers and one sister, so it was a large family indeed. I remember going to my grandparents when I was a kid along with mom and brother. We used to have a great time with everyone so in awe of us as we were from Bangalore. My grandparents used to tell me that dad rarely visited after his father passed away when dad was 25 years and was earning really well. His dad's last day was very interesting. Dad as usual sent him a money order of 25 paise and my granddad had gone to the post office to collect it. After that he went to dad's sister's house and asked for breakfast. While having breakfast he had a heart attack and dad rushed back to the village to do the last rites. Dads mom had passed away when dad was very young and he does not remember her at all. He was mainly brought up by his elder sister but does mention that they struggled to make ends meet, it was extremely difficult and he did not even have slippers to wear to school. They had to walk almost around 6 kilometres one way to school. He rarely took food from home and he always recollected one of his friends' mom for whom he got a job at his hotel who later always packed an extra tiffin for him. Whenever he went to the village which was very rare he would always visit this aunty much more than visit his in-laws. He would not even sit down to rest and always had us book a hotel close by to the village to stay. This village once that treated him badly would now look at him with total respect the little time that he visited. He never though spared me any luxury and I always got what I wanted. He made me study in the most prestigious institutions way beyond his capacity

I lost my dad on the 22nd October 2022 to Lung Cancer. It was an extremely traumatic experience and while I will completely try and keep my emotions at bay I want to ensure that the condition of our medical institutions is understood here and it helps people who go through a similar situation to be alert and take the rightful decisions.

My dad was 76. An extremely healthy man who took care of his well-being and had a diet which I bet cannot be followed by anyone that I have known in my life. His discipline to that diet was strictly adhered to always and never a moment he would sway from it.

He was away from sweets, Aerated drinks, Junk- When I say away – Totally away. Even if I had to offer a chip off a bit from a piece of cake he would refuse. The only exception was on my birthday when he would just take a wee bit of a bite. Once I had asked him why he stayed so away from sweets and he used to mention that as a kid during Diwali everyone would prepare sweets. Due to his family's poverty condition they could not afford it. He used to go to the neighbour's house and stand outside with the hope that someone would hand over something. None did. They just shooed him away. This left a very bad taste with him and he started hating sweets.

However, he was a smoker- An addiction- A habit every one of us have tried to wade him off but could not. I am not saying this is the reason – Because I am given to understand that even Non-smokers get diagnosed with Lung cancer and as explained by many if this was his time then so be it- But MAYBE he would not have struggled so much if he had listened to this advice

It all started when we went to Sakra hospital in November 2021. I took him for a full body check-up. He was asked to "STOP SMOKING" and literally the report had it in Capital letters. He then decided to reduce the number from 7 packets to 3 packets. I remember the doctor saying "Sir – please be careful and stop smoking" Dad replied back "I will reduce the number," and the doctor said – "I did not say reduce, I said "STOP". Dad did get down the number. He used to smoke around 5-6 packets a day and he reduced it to around 3. He ultimately got it further down to 1.

I travelled to the UK during that time and he started deteriorating at home. No one tried to take him to the hospital although he was coughing and they saw immense weight loss. It pains me to write this that MAYBE we could have arrested some pain here.

I remember talking to him on a video call from the UK and he was all wrapped up in a shawl and muffler as he was feeling extremely cold and had a cough. When asked he said this was common and not to bother about it much. He was always happy to talk and sounded cheerful and wanted me to come back home as soon as possible as he was missing me very much. Everywhere I travelled I would keep thinking that this is where I should get dad. I went to the Vatican City and the only prayer I asked to be granted is for my dad to live a long life.

I came back in the month of February and happily hopped home to see the love of my life. I was shocked with what I saw- He had become so frail and was coughing so inconsistently. So, I have this habit of first meeting him at home (Ground floor) and then taking my house keys (Third floor) and then going on top to refresh and come back for breakfast

However, one look at my dad and I was in no mood to go to the third floor. I arrived at around 6 a. m in the morning and got dressed and got ready to take him to the hospital right away. He has never been a person keen to visit hospitals. However, seeing the way, he was struggling he could not manage without medication and wanted a remedy himself.

We went to AP hospital and met a Dr. AS who did not have much time on her hands . She diagnosed dad and wrote it off as Pneumonia and provided medication for the same. I took a chest X-ray which she asked to collect the next day. I did the same and everything was perfectly fine. She also advised us to put him on a Nebulizer . I then came back to Chennai to resume work. His coughing had stopped and he said he was getting better by the day.

Around the 3rd of March I came home again to see him still drained of weight. His cough had reduced but he was looking so poorly and he was facing breathing issues even if he walked for about 10 steps.

He used to always walk for 30 minutes in the morning along with Pranayama which he had stopped due to this breathing issue. I was even more worried, and this time took him to the Bigger AP hospital at Koramangala.

We met Dr. RK who did an initial set of Diagnosis and advised for a few further sets of reports. He also transferred the case to the oncologist. This is the day my life came crashing down in his room when he asked my dad to sit out and wanted to talk to me alone.

He hinted to me that this could be a case of stage 3 Cancer. I could feel the floor under my feet swept off and my life came to a halt . I cried. I still remember dad sitting out innocently without a clue what was wrong. I had   to put up an act of not worrying and stepped out. He had no clue that this was what had happened. I suggested to him that he should have a good meal and we went to Nagarjuna to eat biryani – His favourite meal. He was struggling to walk up the stairs and even laboriously breathing during the wait for the table. I have never seen dad this way. He used to always walk with his chest pushed in front, very strong and firm on his footing. Many would mistake him for an ex-army man. This was scary.

We went home and the next few days were full of tests.

My dad is a kind of person who is very self-sufficient. He will not depend on anyone for anything and let alone disturb me. I never used to feel disturbed but he will always hesitate to ask me for help under the pretext that he is disturbing my work.

However, one day he called me at 4:30 when I was on top floor in the morning stating that he was having difficulty breathing. He was at the hall after finishing his bath and trying very hard to breathe and I had to calm him down and talk smoothly to ensure he stabilizes. Oh, I love him so much!

We finally met Dr. V and Dr. P– The oncologists from AP Koramangala. Again, when I showed him all the reports I had taken he asked dad to sit out and confirmed that it was Lung Cancer. I am still numb with emotions when I write of this now. I called my brother whom I had not spoken to for almost two years and told him this. His response was "I am in a class. I'll call you back" That is when I decided that this is a battle that I will need to fight alone. My brother reconfirmed this feeling afterwards of not even checking at home what was wrong with Appa.

I stayed up long nights looking up on the net , connecting with people and trying to gain as much knowledge as possible. In the meantime, Dr. V had recommended a biopsy for dad. I took dad to AP and dad was so irritated that he refused to do it. He just wanted some medication and wanted to get done with it .

Finally, I convinced him to get a Biopsy done and heard it was a painful process. We were told by Dr. V that after Biopsy he will definitely have to stay under observation wherein he will come and see in for at least minimum six hours and wanted us to book an overnight stay at the hospital. I refused a stay and told him that we will finish and go home. I knew dad will be very uncomfortable to stay at the hospital.

Finally, he wrote us a slip to pay wherein he had mentioned that we have to stay 2-3 days- I went back to him and said we were not even planning to stay for a single day why 2-3 and he replied that this was a protocol.

Due to the fact Dad and I were not willing to stay overnight we asked for an appointment at 10 a. m. We were told that the procedure takes 2 hours and post 6 hours recommended observation we were planning to leave by maximum 8 p. m

We were asked to come to the Bannerghatta centre at 10 a. m and waited till 2 p. m. He had breakfast at 9 a. m and was starving at 2 p. m but it was mentioned that he could not eat. At 2 p. m post multiple calls to Dr. V we finally managed to get the biopsy done and dad was sent back to ward at 4 p. m. Dad was so scared when they wheeled him into the room. I broke down at the reception and the lady gave me a tissue and asked one of the sisters to sit with me. We were there till 8 p. m and absolutely no visit by any doctor except for one nurse who took instructions over the phone. I still cannot understand what was the observation that was recommended earlier. Anyways we went home after this and awaited results post 3 days. Dr. V had mentioned that after the test he would come and visit dad which he never did. This stage itself dad lost hope with this system. He did not even have the courtesy to call up to tell us next steps.

Once we got the report I called up Dr. V and wanted to book an appointment. I requested to see him in Koramangala when he was visiting there but he asked me to come to Bannerghatta. I went over there and booked an appointment from OPD and met him up. This is when we revealed to dad that this is a cancer possibility. Dad did not accept it but in his quiet style kept it to himself. I wanted dad to understand that this was serious. I knew he had an inkling of what was happening as he had completely given up smoking.

Dr. P was also there in the room and they told Dad. We got just around 15 minutes from both to reveal to us that we were in the brink of danger- No time to answer any more questions we had on how this whole thing works. We were advised to have a PET Scan and DR. V had recommended a centre where we decided to visit next week.

We were at that PET scan place at exactly at 6:30 a. m as advised by Dr. V and were told that they open at 7 a. m. We were made to wait at the platform. It was an open space and Dad was shivering due to the cold. There were so many elderly people in the same plight. They opened up at 7 :15 and they took dad into a separate room, put a gown over him and made him wait for almost 3 hrs. They had injected some kind of fluid and provided a bottle to drink water from. He already was someone who used to drink very little water and it was very difficult to gulp down all this water at once

He was then sent to the top room where I was seated in that gown. Please note that he had not had anything to eat from morning but did not seem like anyone cared. People were randomly being selected to finish the PET scan. By the time we were done it was almost 2 p. m. Totally exhausted we went back home and I ordered food for him from outside. He was totally exhausted and mostly irritated by the way the entire thing worked. He felt like everything that was happening was out of his control and he was not very happy about it.

We then waited for the results of the PET scan. However, during this time of wait dad was still struggling with the breathing issue. Once again during this wait he suffered from a bout of breathlessness around 5 a. m. I waited till 9 a. m and then I called Dr. and told him that dads breathing issue is getting worse. I explained to him how badly the incident at the PET scan went about and not a good recommendation from him at all. He said he was at Bannerghatta office and asked me to rush to rushed to Koramangala where Dr. P will be available. He was not even ready to listen to what I was saying. All I was looking for some solution or medication that will help him with this breathing issue till we see a permanent solution.

I rushed to Koramangala with the hope I get to speak to Dr. P and she suggest to me what we can do as next steps for dads breathing problem to subside as they had already met dad. She immediately asked me to book an appointment at reception and come to her cabin and take dad to ward. I told her that I came to ask on next steps and did not get dad at the moment as that was not mentioned earlier. She was very upset that she had to come all this way and I did not book at reception. I told her very clearly that I was not planning to get dad as they have seen him multiple times. She asked me to get the reports and I mentioned to her that it will take time and let me know temporarily a solution for this breathing issue. She asked me to speak to Dr. V in the evening. She also mentioned that I had wasted a lot of her time in having her come to this office.

I called him in the evening and he suggested we go for a Chemo the next day and that was the only solution. I spoke to dad and agreed . He asked us to be there by 7 a. m

Considering what had happened at the PET Scan I requested him if we can come about by 9. Dad was really tired nowadays and slept longer. He said he will have his PA call me and book the appointment. His PA called me to book the appointment and I had requested him that it will be difficult to get my dad up so early as he is already weak . I asked him if I could get him around 9 a. m. Then all was sorted and we were ready to go the next day at 9 a. m. I did message the doctor the reason why I was requesting this change considering the age of my dad.

At around 7 p. m I got a call from his PA stating that he was cancelling the appointment. I was not given any explanation and was asked to speak to the doctor. I called him twice and he did not respond to my calls after that. I was shocked to think that he was upset by my request for a change of time. Was that a little too much to ask?

I am now left with absolutely no option and don't know what to do and the breathing issue continues . At this time my brother (Currently ashamed to call him this) starts screaming and shouting on how I could have taken control of this. How I am interfering with a father -son relationship. I was strong on my side that in the first place I never stopped him from interfering. He stays about 10 steps away from dad's house in the same compound. He wanted to take him to another hospital on that Wednesday where he knew a technician. I tried explaining to him that we need not see a technician but had to see an oncologist. His ego as usual stood in the way and said he knew what he was doing. I then thought through the night and said it's fair for him as he is his father also. I put all his tests so far in a neat file and sent one through WhatsApp and asked him to take him on Wednesday.

On Tuesday afternoon we were expecting him to come and tell us the status on how he is going to take him and no luck. At around 6 p. m I asked him what the plan was as dad would get to bed by 8. He then tells me he can't take him as he has college work. I asked him – could he not have told us earlier? Now I had nowhere to go. It was too late in the night for me to look for alternatives or book any other appointments. This was something I wanted to attend to asap as I did not want him to suffer from the breathing problem any more. One of dad's friends had then suggested Kidwai. I then took him to Kidwai on a Friday morning at 9 a. m.

At the outset the place was brimming with so many people. Everywhere it was just people and more people. I was asked to fill a form and provide my Dad's Aadhar card which we had not brought along with us. I made my dad sit at the reception who was already tired at this moment of walking from the gate till the OPD (Autos not allowed).

The staff were extremely rude and not helpful (Did not expect either from the Government hospital but did not think it will be so bad)

I asked them if they could help me print the Aadhaar copy from my phone and they refused. I had to travel almost 2 kms in an auto to take this print out and come back. I now submitted and went to pay the fees in the billing. After waiting for 30 minutes in this queue and giving them a slip I was provided by the enquiry centre. The lady at the billing office told me that the income column was blank. I told them that I already mentioned while registering that I had provided the information to the counter and requested her to add on the slip. She got really offended and said that was not her job. I had to go back to the registration, add that on and come back, waited again for 30 minutes in the queue and paid.

During this time my dad was super exhausted and it was almost 1 p. m. Doctors had left and would be back only by 4 p. m. One he did not have the energy to wait till 4 p. m and secondly, he did not like this place and we decided to leave to come back on Tuesday as the doctors came only twice a week.

The days that passed by were hell. I could sense dad falling into that silence and nervousness as he was not aware of what was happening in his body, He had also stopped having his contemporary daily drink. He was trying to get back into the routine of Pranayama and running in the morning but was getting exhausted in the process.

Finally, Tuesday morning arrived and we walked in at 8, the time they opened . There was a long queue and people of all ages were waiting there and had even put their slippers onto the queue. It was mayhem again. There was one security guard who was so rude to everyone and shouting for absolutely no reason. Considering that the set of people who were waiting here were actually the ones who were struggling to save their lives was ironic . They did not deserve this kind of treatment at all.

It was a horrible scene when they opened up almost 30 minutes late. Everyone rushed in pushing and pulling elderly and even some handicapped people. The security ushered everyone inside without being sensitive to the fact that he was rushing people who were in wheelchairs also. We were sent into a room which was occupied by around two students who read our reports. They stepped out and got an opinion from a senior doctor. This kept happening for almost 30 minutes. They then wrote down a few more tests we have to do. I told them that we had already done these tests just about a week back. They mentioned that even if all tests are done it is their protocol to have it done at their hospital again. We could not imagine going through the drama of repeating all the tests once again. Especially dad being a person whose patience level was very low he was at the brink of saying that he was giving up and all of this was a bogus.

We came out and dad had to sit down on the chair below because he was super tired and could not walk. When I think of all of this now – My blood boils to think how much more we could have avoided this pain and agony to him by just being nice. I tried to convince him that this hospital might not work out for us. Going through this every time after we started treatment will be very difficult to handle. I started to think on what do these people take when they leave this world. What does it cost them to just be nice people? We then took a call to never go back to KIDWAI again as we have lost the confidence on how they would further handle this.

My dad has always been someone who hated hospitals and medicines and I was surprised that he was keen to check in at the Ph hospital and take an opinion there. This went on to show how much trouble he must have been having and how unbearable it was for him.

I took him to a doctor. He mentioned that he visited a few years back and was super impressed with him along with all the reports. He saw all of the reports and suggested we see an oncologist as he is unable to decipher anything. He checked if dad smoked a lot and I started complaining about it. Dad said that he has now completely stopped and also has stopped his limited drinks. While we were about to leave he asked me to stay back and told me that at first glance the reports did not look fine at all and my dad had very little time. I broke down and told him that I will try and get him out of this as much as I can. He said it's better I let my dad eat and drink what he wants till he is fine. He said he will pray for us and that is all that he was capable of doing

As of now there are no options and I had to act quickly. One contact was provided by the doctor I saw in AP who suggested that his grandmother was getting treated here and was less expensive than AP. I had not explored this option as yet but decided to now go for it. A lot of friends also suggested other places like Manipal, Shimoga doctor, HCG, BGS etc. I decided to go to this place as it seemed a small player but was told the doctor was from Manipal. I called the doctor the day before and his secretary called me back to book the appointment and we got it for the next day which was a Thursday.

Before going to the hospital, I messaged the doctor requesting him to firstly install some confidence in dad so that he trusts the treatment and he agreed to do it. He did speak to dad very well and gave us a few options of doing Chemo. As a secondary thought we decided to check also in HCG – One of the biggest names in cancer treatment in Bangalore. As it was close by dad was ok to go there also. We then took the auto to HCG and waited for almost the rest of the day to make a bill payment and get a doctor's appointment. The doctor also suggested a few Chemos but with a different schedule. While the M hospital offered us 4-6 sessions of Chemos with a 21-day gap in between whereas HCG offered us of three cycles of 7 days in between and three times more the price of Hospital M

We came back home as dad wanted time to decide what options to take. It was not the cost that I was worrying about. I knew after quite a research that Chemos were pretty painful and the way I was seeing different hospitals I did not have to go through waiting and struggles during the process of the treatment itself.

During this time, I was trying to see how I could manage the funds for what was coming my way. I knew dad would be wanting to pay for all this. However, I wanted it to be the least of his worries at this moment. During the year beginning I remember reading a mail from my organization that if I did not want to change the composition of dad's contribution from my last year enrolment I need not do anything on the tool. Hence, I did not worry but however tried to login to check if all was intact, I had difficulty in logging in and raised a ticket. This ticket was not looked into for almost a month and by the time they came back to me the window to enroll was closed. I fought a battle I lost. I gave up as I had to concentrate on more important aspects at home.

I was keen to go for the 21-day gap one as that will help him get some recovery between sessions. He was extremely stressed and it was so painful to see him contemplate on what needs to be done. I left it completely to him to take a call. If M then we were to start by Saturday and HCG on Monday. He said he wanted to think of the options and we left it at that. During that weekend we made a conscious effort not to talk anymore of hospitals and cancer and medicines. In the last one and half month we were only talking of this in the house. We ordered some good food over the weekend and had a quiet jolly time. However, I knew there was so much tension building inside him on what was to come by. The doctors had told him what would happen during the chemo sessions and he was definitely not looking forward to it at all.

Such a healthy , active person now in this dilemma was something I am still remembering with a deeply wounded heart. Surprisingly he was up and about the next day with his walking and breathing exercises. He again said he decided to overcome this by himself. I just loved him . So, determined on everything.

The Monday that came by we decided to go ahead with Hospital M. In the meantime, I had sleepless nights reading through what this chemo was all about and I did not like what I read through. I was praying that dad is not affected to that extent by the side effects. I know for a fact that due to his eating habits and discipline his immunity was very good. Hoping this was going to save him from the side effects.

We went and met the doctor and dad was very quiet. Dad has always been someone who would not open up much about his emotions. I have only seen his eyes tearing up when I leave for Chennai from Bangalore. However not once would he ask me to stay back as he knew I was going back to my work and it was important, that was an indication of the amount of love he had for me. I still remember him dropping me at the bus stop and smoking a cigarette and waiting for however long it took for the bus to come before he bade me Goodbye. He had a strange way of showing his love. He would never expressively open up about how much he cared. In his strange little ways, he would make it known that I was his life. When I met his friends all they would say is how he keeps talking about me and how proud he was of what I made of my life. Yes- One nagging thought was the fact that I remained single. I at some point wanted to get married and have a life as everyone else. This ritual of boys visiting home and then making it once every week drama really put me off and I went into the mode of saying No even before I saw the prospect. Only when I moved over to Chennai did this stop. He did get the most influential guys to the house. The family was at the top notch but somehow the boy did not take to my fancy. Our priorities never matched. Dad would never force me into anything. It was always my choice. Once I did get engaged only to be broken after a while due to some complications. That's when I had decided this is how I had to lead my life. I never complained. My travel was my therapy. I have a huge crowd of friends and a large group who keep me busy with all the weekends completely packed with activities.

We went there on April 14th 2022 and got the first Chemo done. He was very quiet not knowing what to expect. I was working on my laptop during this time. He felt very sleepy and slept throughout the injection of the medicines prescribed by the doctor. Even though we had started with this Chemo we were still awaiting results of another Lung molecular test from the biopsy sample which I collected back from AP. Apparently this test result will help us fine tune the treatment and target results even better was what the doctor had mentioned. I was managing an extremely difficult project and was managing work along with the project and trying to do justice to both. My first priority was obviously my dad. I worked around the office with his needs on top . A girl called Dolma was extremely friendly and did a great job in putting dad at ease and relaxed him. Dad put up a very strong face and braved it out without a clinch. After the diagnosis he had generally gone very quiet and has not reacted too much. He did show his dissatisfaction for being taken from one place to another. It did not hit him that he has cancer and was hoping that this is something he can overcome by willpower as he has always been doing till now.

We came back home and he seemed to be carrying on perfectly fine and was in good spirits. I had already explained to him post my reading on net and speaking to various friends that the side effects could be as follows:

1. Loss of appetite
2. Hair fall
3. Constipation
4. Loose motions
5. Body pain
6. Burning sensation were some of the main ones I had warned him against.

He was never someone who read the net or even knew how to use an Android. In fact, he only started using the normal button cell phone after I had forced him onto it. Even though being so super smart, he had this mind block against technology and when I tried to teach him sometimes he would just ask me to stop. He would just know how to answer calls and make calls. Not even store phone numbers.

The second day he was super tired. His saturation seemed to have gone to around 80 and he was having great difficulty breathing. I called up the doctor (S) and he told me to get him to the clinic where he was practising (Hospital A at Wilson Garden) .I forced dad to come along. He was refusing and it was a difficult time to get him to the hospital. This was a very tough time I had during his treatment. I almost thought I was losing my dad as his breathing was so laborious

Once there we were asked to wait for a really long time. I told them that dad had breathing trouble and it did not make any difference to them. To them it was important that I finish the registration first. I made my dad wait outside as the reception area was full. Corona was still rampant and I did not want dad to get affected by it. In the meantime Dr. S told me that he had left to another hospital I was surprised as I thought he would at least try and find out the issue especially as he had administered the Chemo. He had coordinated with another lady doctor who was attending a meeting and was asked to wait for a longer period. In this time, we had put him on to oxygen and his saturation was gradually improving and he was also starting to look much better than before. Then the lady doctor came in and she was a very sweet caring lady who spoke to dad very well and told him how these things can be common in Chemo treatments. This was so important to dad as a major part of the treatment was that he was convinced he was doing it for his benefit. I was nevertheless shocked to understand that a lot of things are more important in the hospital than actually caring for the patient himself. We took him home feeling much better.

This difficulty he was having in breathing really made me scared. The next day onwards the loose motions started. He felt very drained and was finding it difficult even getting out of bed. He slowly started reducing the food intake. When asked he said that he had lost all sense of taste and could not eat anything. He used to go to the restroom room at least 10-11 times a day. He was losing even the little he was eating/ He would refuse a bedpan or diaper as it made him very uncomfortable. Even to pass urine he had to go to the restroom. It was more so his ego to show that he was not bedridden.

While he started sleeping most of the time it was getting difficult to have him eat food as he lost his appetite and taste and started drastically losing weight. The days passed by with him just going down the energy drain. He never shared the pain and trouble he was going through with anyone. I was happy at least he was able to move around and manage things by himself. He was already someone who drank very less water even when he was fine and now he completely stopped with the fear that this might increase the loose motions.

It was a confusing phase. He had to eat to fight the effects of the medicine but he could not. He had to take a lot of rest and was told that he would sleep a lot, but then sometimes he just slept without eating a morsel of food. I tried convincing him that drinking water will hydrate him and it's important for the chemo to work. He would not budge even a bit. It was a very difficult phase for me. I had a few friends who stuck to me during these hard times- I can clearly call out my ex-colleagues Rajesh, Aruna, Kalpana, Pooja and a few more who called me to see in everything was going on fine. They would be on long calls with me to ensure I remained strong and giving me tips on how to handle this. These were friends who were in some form or other providing or provided the same kind of support to someone in the family.

Aruna offered me an option of actually going the ayurvedic route and she and her husband were so kind to me to guide me on this path. I spoke to dad to see if we can take this option. I was ready to go to any extent to ensure we avoid this Chemo and get him to recover. Rajesh suggested an alternative I can try. Dad refused any of the options. Not that he liked the chemo process but he has always been a person who is less explorative. Even when he used to drive me to the bank on his bike he would just finish the bank work and come back. If we had another task and I would insist that we finish that also he would say to do it another day.

There was a friend of his who came home and also suggested the Shimoga doctor who had actually done miracles in the field of Cancer/ move him to Chennai etc. Dad did not budge. I was ready to even fly him out if he had just said ok. He just said that he wanted to see how this Chemo worked out and then later take a call. He did not want to get involved in a lot of things at the same time. I totally understood his situation and let it be.

So, we continued to go the Chemo route. The date for the second Chemo came in. Dad was slowly recovering but I realized that he was getting nervous as the dates started to near. He would suddenly go all quiet again and it was almost like he was wondering how the second chemo would go.

We went back to Hospital M for the second Chemo. Dad has always been someone who would want perfection in the way he dressed and looked. Not one hair out of place. Shirt and pant neatly ironed out. When we got ready to go to the Chemo he was refusing to wear the pants even and was ok with the Lungi. Such was the pain and discomfort he was suffering from this entire process.

I had to get him an oxygen concentrator to help with the variations in breathing pattern. We were using this for around two hours a day as suggested by the doctor. We were maintaining at 2 litres and also on Nebulizer. This seemed to be helping in getting him out of the breathing problem issue he was facing in the first place and this was a relief indeed

By this time, he had stopped having his bath as it was very cold and also rarely brushed his teeth. During the first few days of the Chemo the effects were severe and he slept through it. It will take around 10 days to settle down and then he was weak and very low on energy.

He hated this phase. He has always been so active getting up at 2 in the morning to check on the water, starting the day by 5. But now he rarely even gets up from bed. Such were the effects of the treatment. It was really painful to see him going through this.

I had completely moved base to Bangalore- However I was to shift the old house by the end of May, hence I came to Chennai for three days to complete searching for the house. When I used to look for houses in Chennai I would always look for a place keeping dad's comfort in mind. I would love him to visit me and have a great stay. This time also I did the same. I could not find any for the first two days. Only got my car banged by a Tempo traveller and had to leave it in the garage for repairs. I did not tell anything to dad as I knew in this condition he would get very worried. The last day however I fixed the place and went back home,

Ideally dad would be very keen on knowing where I took the house, rent, directions etc. However, this time he was too much in a different mode to check on all these details. I anyway told him all about my search and the new house details without the car accident part. I had told him that I will get the car at least back to Bangalore so that it will be easy for us to move around and not be dependent on these cabs and he said that it was not necessary.

The result of the LMT was apparently not very good. The doctor could not see what he called a" Mutation" which made the treatment very complicated. Earlier he had suggested targeted therapy but now decided against it. During this time, I had got the salon guy home to give him a good shave as he was not in a position to walk up to their place as he usually used to do every first Sunday of the month. He was sitting in the backyard while I was working in the front room. After finishing the guy left and dad came back into the room. I was shocked to see that he had shaved his hair completely head and I did not like it even a bit. He said he was scared of seeing his hair falling and thought this was easier to maintain. There was nothing to be done now but I was not at all happy about this. It made him look so weak and vulnerable.

I could clearly say that dad was out of his prime self. This went on till we completed the four chemos. Each one took a toll on his body and he got weaker and weaker and even sadder. He had also become very dull and quiet. As stated earlier he was always someone who never spoke much of his emotions and feelings. He now even stopped speaking of his pain. I used to love the way his face would abruptly break into a smile or laugh if he found something funny and then go back to being quiet quickly.

While Dr. S was consulted earlier he had mentioned 4-6 Chemos. After every Chemo we were given an injection to be administered after 24 hrs. I always booked Portea and had them administer this injection. The last two times I had asked for a private person to come in and do it. Apparently, this injection controlled the side effects of the chemo. I was glad that apart from the loose motions he did not have any other side effects. I did not see hair fall as much as he was worried. But I knew he was not feeling all that well without showing it out much.

At this stage he was not in need of this concentrator any more. It was such a great feeling having to send off the concentrator. It was leaving us both with a sense of achievement. We celebrated by ordering food from outside for this. He was now maintaining the saturation without the help of the concentrator.

We finished the fourth one and I would say again how he was very fortunate to have not had many of the side effects like Body pain, Body burning etc as he was already quite stressed with the issue of Loose motions. Now when we finished 4th doctor had suggested a PET scan and we got ready for that .

The earlier time was a bad experience and we were expecting the same. This time the difference was that he was weaker and less on energy than the last time. It was such a pitiable sight to see him sit and wait outside for the PET scan time to be nearing. Again, the impatience and irritation he was having. Considering what he was going through it was understandable. As we were taking treatment in this place we were given precedence over the rest and were treated much better than the last time. The time spent unnecessarily waiting was just the same as these guys had just one machine for everyone

However, the happy thing was he did not have much breathing trouble when walking up like he used to have during earlier chemos. His breathing trouble had definitely stopped. It was a relief to see him move quickly without waiting for breaks. He also managed to walk from the house to the end of the lane for the cab. Our lane was quite constricted and being a dead end was always trouble for the cab guys to take a turn after they picked or dropped us. But earlier when he was unable to walk we had to get the can to the house without any choice. In earlier instances before his sickness he would prefer to even walk to the nearby banks and close works to be completed.

When we completed the tests the doctor immediately gave us the results via WhatsApp message. There was improvement but the cancer was not definitely gone. It was almost 70% improvement. We consulted him on next steps and what can be done to reduce that 30%. The doctor over the message was clearly saying that the lump was still there.

There were a few options he gave. We were to complete the two remaining two chemos Go for immunotherapy or settle in for tablets. He said that the immunotherapy would cost us around 1. 5 lakhs a month and we will need to administer till the time the lump dissolves.

While I was in for the first two options he did not guarantee that the immunotherapy will solve the problem for sure, he was saying that it's all a touch and go option. In cancer there is no guarantee of any of the treatments that they undertake and it's not about what the cost of the treatment would be. It all depends on how the body reacts to the drugs that are administered. Dad wanted to go for the tablets option. I was not keen on that at all and the doctor was also saying that tablets are the least sure of all the options.

He refused any further chemo. He said he did not have the energy and the mental strength to take any more chemos. I could not say anything further. Till now he would quietly sit and listen to whatever the doctor said. Most of the time the doctor would be on the mobile and I would just wish that he looks up and gives some respect and time for dad and hears him out. I found this very rude to an elderly person. We did not have any choice though. He was a good man though.

This time dad spoke for around 15 minutes but was so clear on what he was saying and so convicted of his message. I was stunned but super proud of him. He said that he was ok if his time was coming nearer. So, we took the tablets and went home. I was not happy.

During this time, we managed to take him to a friend's daughter's wedding. Although my brother was going to the same event he did not bother to even take my dad in his health condition. I managed to book a cab and take him there. My brother's family now behaved as they did not know us. Even after it started raining and he was sitting out in the cold waiting for a cab to come and take us home. I in fact told dad that he could go in the car and I would come in the cab. Dad was quite jolly at this time and this memory of both of us sitting outside and chatting away to glory will be etched in my mind forever as good memories.

When dad's friends started visiting him, they all started advising him to finish the remaining two chemos. He was on the tablets for the 10th day now. They were urging him that he has come so far why not just get it done with, they also mentioned the fact that tablets will not be effective. He did not have any side effects from the tablet but he did say that he was still feeling tired and drowsy most of the time. He started taking care of stuff around the house as normal and I also went to Chennai to set up my place and settle down things. I was a little more relaxed and was hoping that things were slowly coming back to what it was.

He was coming under pressure to finish the 5th and 6th and also, I think he started feeling much better which made him decide to finish up the remaining 2. This time I did not put him under any pressure at all. It was his own choice to complete the 2. He wanted to go back to M for consultation.

While I took him only for this purpose to speak to the doctor and take the next course he was already prepared for the chemo. I was glad he was doing it without compulsion as then I would feel very guilty about it. We finished the chemo and came back home. Now we almost knew the drill and knew what the side effects would be.

However, this time the side effects were even worse. We were not sure why. He really struggled this time and weight started dropping again.

The loose motions were getting bad. I even tried reiki healing this time. The first time I got an external practitioner to try remote healing on him, this person advised me that in this case they would need healing on a daily basis. I started researching options on how I can learn and do it for myself . I got a slot in Chennai for two days and with my friend driving down to Chennai I blocked this slot. I was feeling bad to leave him for two days but wanted to take up this class to ensure I am able to help with that daily healing that would help him.

I came home and practiced on him. I had only done the basic course and prayed that this would somehow ease out the pain to some degree at least .

There was one incident that put Appa into stress during this period. He always kept his cupboard keys very very carefully. One reason being he had my jewellery locker key in it. As I had made him responsible for it – he made sure he kept it really careful. Secondly, he always gave this feeling that there were some documents which were very important. One time when I was sitting in the front room and doing my work I came out from the bathroom quite tense . He had dropped the key into the bathroom. He had it in his pocket and while he got up from the Indian toilet that he was using it fell out of the pocket. It disturbed me totally to see him in this state. I took a long wire and put it into the toilet pipeline to pull out the key but did not get anything. I then put all forms of feelings away from my head and did this for my dad. I put my hand deep down the pipe and luckily found the key. Dad was so relieved. That was his heart.

His eating habits also had changed. He now started eating strange things that he never used to eat before. I was happy. He had ice creams and sweets and a lot of junk. At Least this way there were some calories that were going into the body. As he did not suffer from any complications of sugar or Cholesterol I did not try to control these cravings. He also at one time had wine which the doctor had mentioned will not be a problem. We had brought this wine for his birthday. He wanted to visit Chikkathirupathi for the second time post his illness. The first time we went was to post his first Chemo and I had a fight with him for which I still feel guilty about. It was a fight for him to again eat the right amount of food and he refused. But it did not last for long. Fights with him after his illness did not last for long. I would always come back and talk to him unlike before where I would not talk for days even though he would come and try to break the ice.

We went now for his birthday for the second time. He was able to walk up this time with ease to the temple. We also grabbed some lunch from outside and got it home. These moments are the most precious for me which will stay with me forever.

At some point of time I do remember his facing issues with constipation. Toilet habit was something dad was very particular about. He was very clean about it and was particular about passing motion daily.

We tried relieving the motion problem via various natural methods as the doctor had advised us in giving him any tablets due to his chemo. This was a big problem at this time. Along with this was the fact that he was not sleeping well at night.

He slept throughout the day and maybe was the cause he could not fall asleep at night. He did sometimes try to be awake in the mornings but we could see that he was really struggling to do this and would doze off. We could also not give him any tablets for the sleep as again it would interfere with his Chemo treatment. We were giving him a lot of fluids as his taste buds had still not returned. He did like his mutton leg soup and he went back to having this regularly every day. We thought this was good enough to keep him going. Apart from this we gave him Kanji and Manna drink regularly along with Protein powder.

Once we were done with the 6th Chemo the doctor said that he will put him on maintenance. He did not advice a PET scan hence we did not get any done. This was secretly good news for me as I read that maintenance happens once the chemos are done and we are able to sustain the disease together with maintenance. He administered an Injection for maintenance and advised that in the beginning we should give him this twice a month and then move to once a month. Even this time he did not have much time to talk to us without spending time on his mobile

We came back home with the happy feeling that not any more chemos were required. At this time, he was able to walk around and eat slightly better. We were hopeful that from here onwards we will slowly try to build his energy and strength and get him back to speed.

He asked for the monthly meeting of his association to be conducted for August. This was held at our house at the association room they had separately built for themselves. The last time they had this meeting was in February and post that the president who was very close to dad fell sick. He had suffered a stroke and was admitted in ICU for a while before he was brought home. This brought a shock to dad. This uncle was an Ex- military man and also a hockey coach. Even at this age he was extremely active and was not showing any symptoms of illness at all. The fact that such a strong man suffered a stroke was quite shocking to him. Although he was brought home he died two days before Dad's fourth Chemo. When I got to hear about this from his son I had requested all the association members not to tell this to dad as it might Psychologically affect the chemo.

To attend the meeting dad walked up the entire stairs and he was super proud of himself as he could do it without much difficulty. Another feather in the cap.

Another moment of pride when the Locality association members invited dad as the chief guest for the flag hoisting on Independence Day. He just refused to do it and said he is not comfortable. I was asked to come into the room and convince him to agree. I told dad that this is something he deserved. He had done so much for this locality and most of the time without even taking money and spending from his own pocket. He had laid the entire road. He had also done a safety construction at our village temple for which he had contributed a lot of money. He never used to put up a fight for money at any money and was content and happy with what he had. He let go of property that he had to get as part of his father's share and also as part of my mother's share. Finally, we made him agree for the event and went about trying to decide what he has to wear. I took him on the bike and he was treated with such respect by all the members there. They were shocked to see him in this state as it was a while after his sickness that he had stopped attending the meetings. He was always someone you would find shying away in all the photos and never taking the forefront at all. This was a huge honour for him indeed. While I was getting him back he was saying that this was very embarrassing for him and I tried to convince him saying that was not the case. It was a moment of pride and honour for him. Not everyone got this.

With dad on the recovery symptoms I came to Chennai to start getting things to normalcy with work. This was around the first week of August, I planned to stay for two weeks and then get back home. During this time, I got to know that dad was not keeping well again and was taken to the hospital by my niece. I'm really worried now. Also, I was informed that he needed a wheelchair.

Till now whatever breathing trouble he had he would walk slowly but get angry if anyone offered a wheelchair so when I knew he did take one I realized that he must be really struggling to walk, I was on line with my niece constantly to monitor what was happening. He was apparently administered oxygen and sent back with a few tablets to be taken. He had met a general OPD doctor (A name I do not want to mention) at hospital PH. I realized that it is better I get back to Bangalore and go back home. I realized that one person that I trusted will look after him in my absence. My niece was not doing what she should be. Especially after all the sacrifice my dad did for her. I remember him dropping her off to college every day and these included days that he was sick. He used to take her around for getting her licence and pan card also done. To the extent that he actually created a bank account for both of them to ensure that they saved money and started putting money into those accounts. He did a lot more than this. I might never be able to cover all that here. Somehow both of them forgot all this during his treatment and were not even able to look after him during my short absence.

When my niece took him to the hospital when I was in Trichy he told me when I came back how very impatient she was and never waited for him to voice out what he wanted. He was very disappointed and also wanted me to collect the bike key which he had handed over to her. I never did

When I saw dad, he was not keeping well . He was also sleeping a lot and not in the best of spirits at all. He also complained of breathing problems. I decided to take him to the doctor again to check up. I knew he would not be comfortable at M with Dr. S who did not bother to look up most of the time from his mobile and I was surprised never bothered to follow up to find out how he was doing. I took him to St. J which was one place that he would always talk high of and registered him for consultation. He still wanted a wheelchair here. It was tearing my heart to see him wait for a cab so tiredly in that wheelchair. I was the last to rush for registration and I had to leave him alone at the waiting desk and come back to pick him up for the appointment.

When we got our turn to see the doctor we were ushered into a room. In this room sat two students who took the reports and reviewed it. They made some notes and then called in the senior doctor. He looked at dad like he was an outcaste. I told him that we have always been coming to StJ regularly and I decided to get him here. I also told him that we had already administered six chemos and he questioned as to why we did that outside when StJ was the family hospital and why get him here now. I told him dad was comfortable coming here now. He looked at dad and said that he can't do anything for him now as he is very weak. Neither did he look at the reports nor ask any questions on what help he wanted . He told me to get him to eat well and get him back after a week. I felt really bad for dad as he sat there listening to this compassionate review of the reaction from the doctor. I understand that doctors are busy but is it not important that you treat the people who come to see you with some love and affection?

I took him out and we went home. I don't know what was going through dad's mind but I was devastated. While he was about to sleep in the night I asked him if we should go to PH the next day. Ph has been another hospital that has always been close to Dad's heart. I was surprised when he nodded his head and said Yes. In earlier circumstances considering his dislikes of doctors and hospitals he would have definitely asked to be left alone. That was the pain he was going through and wanted to get cleared of this.

Next day again we got ready and went to Ph. We waited for almost an hour after the designated time of appointments and met Dr. R. We were there at 8 for the appointment and the doctor was met at 10 a. m. Dad had not eaten anything at this time and was feeling hungry a bit. Here also he had to be ushered into a wheelchair as he was finding it difficult to walk by himself .

Dr. R gave us a very good feel - Most importantly he gave dad time. He learnt about the entire history of the case. He told me that dad is very weak at this moment and will not be ready for any further treatments. He wanted to ensure that his strength improved . He gave me a few tablets and asked me to take him back home. Post the consultation I thought I will take him to the cafeteria for him to eat something. While I said we can sit inside he insisted that he sit in the wheelchair outside and have his food. I did lose my patience a bit here but recouped myself and gained strength to handle him with care. He wanted to have a Bisibele bath – after a long time he actually asked for something specific and it was not available. I got him Idlis and they were not at all edible. Dad ate one mouth and spat it out and we had to leave it to the dogs. I could not blame him as it was really bad.

In this instance he saw a man far off and said "Fish man" I did not understand. That other guy got uncomfortable with my dad staring at him and I asked him what was the problem. Dad said he knew this guy when the hotel was open and recollected meeting him last around 15 years back. What a memory! I really thought dad was mistaken as the other man did not even bat an eyelid out of recognition. To avoid any further embarrassment, I went up to him and explained who we were and he said he did not recognize my dad. I then mentioned Dad's hotel "Thevar's canteen" and he then recollected and was shocked to see how dad had changed so much. He was feeling sad that he was reduced to this kind of a shape and size

We kept him on those tablets but noticed that dad was getting more tired by the period. His eating was also bad. I was getting worried on how I will increase his energy and started putting across various ideas to ensure I try and work on.

At this time there was a need for me to be in Trichy for a week. While I was worried about leaving dad back I was not of any help being at home also as he slept most of the time. I decided to finish this trip and come back to take him to Ph again for the next steps. Now when I think of it – Maybe just sitting along with him when he was sleeping and holding his hands might have been of a great help itself.

I realized that dad felt comfortable with R and thought it would be best to take the course of action from him. Before I left I told his second wife to ensure to monitor and keep the saturation level above 90. Also, to check weight daily and BP also.

While I was hoping that my niece would help her, she almost either forgot to check weight or stopped responding to my calls. Dad at this moment stopped picking his phone as he could not run to get to it and it started to feel heavy in his hand too and my only source of communication to his health was his second wife, she kept telling me she is recording the weight and the saturation so I was rest assured that nothing was amiss.

I went to this temple in Trichy to pray for Dad's health and was very confident that nothing will happen to him and he will get better soon.

When I returned home and was devastated again to see him go really poorly. I checked the records to see that he had gradually lost weight and his saturation was wavering between 80-84. I yelled at this lady and told why she did not tell me it was bad. She kept assuring me that she was recording it every day.

When I went back I did not know what to do. I was asked by R to do a blood test the week after and get him for the next course of action. I took the test and went by myself as I did not want to tire dad.

The day before I had also taken him to the ENT as he complained of his ear getting blocked. We actually made around three trips to the ENT and finally told him to clean it out as it was getting very difficult. The doctor told us that he cannot do it and tried giving us some ointment for the third time. He said that if he cleaned it now dad would faint and would need to be admitted. Dad had done this cleaning process before and was not scared of it so we told him that we will bear that risk and to go ahead. It was a simple process and all the wax was cleaned out and dad was much better. Another annoying aspect that was sorted. At this moment my biggest regret was making dad wait as I was stuck on an office call trying to help another team member and poor dad sitting on the stool and waiting patiently for me to finish the call

When I went to R. He looked at the report and said that it seemed fine and we can look at putting him through further treatment. This was a mild form of Chemo but not

Chemo entirely. So, the next day I got him to the hospital and took him to the general ward. They did a check but saw that his saturation was very low and immediately put him on the oxygen concentrator and administered him with some fluids to give him some energy. Post this we asked him to move to the Chemo ward as the doctor had mentioned that the chemo can start after two days.

When the doctor came to see him after two days he said that dad is still weak and we cannot take any further steps. Its better we move him away from the Chemo ward to general, administer his health for a while and then discuss next steps. I was just worried on the fact that we were just losing time

We kept him in observation for a while and then took him home. At this stage he was almost bedridden and could not move around at all. He was not even able to get to the toilet to pass urine or stools. However, he used to have a constant urge to pass urine and was provided tablets for the same. For the stools he used to just sit down from the bed. His second wife used to keep making a noise every time he passed stools in the room and made a face at him. She kept washing everything that he used to wear saying it was making the room stink. This was a huge inconvenience for dad and made him feel so dirty about himself. I used to step in many times and ask her to let him be.

He was at home at this stage for about a week. I took the blood test again and took back the reports and now this time along with dad to Rajeev. While we went to the general ward for admission they sensed that his saturation was still low and advise to be admitted to the ICU. While I was not keen on this the earlier general physician who saw him said that it is risky and we have to admit him in ICU.

This is not what I had expected when I got him down. I agreed and they took him over. He was so petrified of the ICU and was not keen at all. Also, they had strict rules on timings when we could go and see him.

So, I spent the entire day sitting outside the waiting room desperate to know what was happening inside and how he was doing.

They did not even allow you to stand outside the door to check on how he was. No doctors answered your queries as they were busy and mostly short staffed with few trainee doctors attending to a lot of patients.

I was told that he was admitted due to a blood infection When I wanted to know why they said that this was normal for a patient going through Chemo. At this time, I realized that the doctor conducting the chemo should have been clear of all this and did not explain this to a large extent. It was due to the fact his saturation dropped. The lung specialist then questioned me as to why I did not have him on the concentrator . I then told him that last time when I came to the general physician to this hospital I was not advised to have him on the concentrator . He said that was not the right thing to do as he should be on the concentrator for longer periods.

So, at this time I got the concentrator ordered back at home. I was informed that a 5 litre should work and we were giving him only till 2 litres. They had pumped in some medicine and were happy to hear the news that the next day they could move him to a semi- ICU as he was recovering.

During this period, I slept at night in the waiting room and I was being called continuously to buy medicines from the pharmacy. I remember at this time even though I could not identify the medicines I purchased a very similar looking tube at least three times. When I questioned at the pharmacy they told me that they will give what products are entered onto the system. Then a slip with a particular number is provided to you and you will need to go and buy that for the doctors.

So, I was called almost three times and I would rush to the ICU to be told to get the medicines. During the evening visiting hours for which I was desperately waiting I was sent to see him and was shocked with what I saw.

The place was almost like a fish market. I was told by the PRO that the ICU will have a separate nurse for each person along with a doctor. Here it was a crazy place with so many trainees running around, monitors screaming and it was freezing. I was further shocked to see my dad who was wearing a gown but was half way down his chest and had nothing to cover him or save him from the cold.

He is already someone who would not bear the cold for long and to see him like this shivering my heart just died. He will never sit in rooms with AC on and also hated when I booked AC trains for him to travel from Bangalore to Chennai. At home he would need two blankets to sleep in. He was almost in tears and told me that he was freezing. I called the nurse and asked her what the hell was happening. She apologized and then went around getting a blanket for him

There were so many wires around him and he was wrapped up in monitors. All he wanted was to get out of this place. I told him that we should be out of this place in one day. But it was nice to see that he was not in any pain or anything. He was irritated with all the wires pinned to his body, I also was told that they had injected his hand many times for blood tests and stuff like that.

If there was any chance I could have transferred that suffering from dad I would have happily done so. It was also so difficult to act happy and jolly and behave that all is well with so many emotions killing me internally. I used to always go somewhere alone and cried all by myself. Most of the time I just wanted to scream out loud and beg that god to get him out of this misery and get him well soon. But I had to do it. I joked and laughed for a while with him and went out to let his second wife in to see him. By the time I came later I could see that he was warmed up with a heater set up next to him.

That night I came home as it did not make sense sleeping in that waiting room and he was declared fine to be moved to Semi- ICU the next day. I spoke to a friend of mine from whom I got to know that the doctor who was seeing my dad was actually her brother-in -law . This gave me some happiness as now I know I can ask to have him taken care of specially.

The next morning when I was getting ready to leave for the hospital I got a call from the security saying the nurse was calling me. I was super scared. I asked him if all was ok and he said that he did not know. I rushed to the hospital in a panic mode to learn that they had called me to tell me to buy medicines. I did ask the nurse that it would have been really helpful if they mentioned that when they called out for us and we would not get so worried. I was waiting patiently for him to be moved to the Semi ICU.

This is apparently a place where around 6 persons will be housed and visiting doctors and nurses will be stationed. While the visiting hours were flexible we still had to adhere to it. The good thing about this place was that it had fewer machines and systems around and much less noisy and the best thing – NO AC around. I ensured dad was settled in well and he looked very distraught and weak. I keep having this pain strike through me every time I look at him in this manner. But I had no choice and I was trying my best to get him back to health. With the help of the known doctor I managed to secure a bit of a leniency on the visiting hours and met him quite often. The hospital provided food which was supposed to be fed by the nurses. Only thing is that they did not feed the patients. They were so busy in managing their accounts and records that the people in the beds were the last priority. I was amazed to see how busy they were making their numerous records and studies. I would think that while this is all important but the people in the room lying down for treatment were much more important.

We were again called in regularly to ensure that we purchased the medicines and came. Once I remember that dad wanted to go to the toilet and he refused to go in the bed pan. I asked the help of this male nurse and he literally turned back from his notes and asked me to wait for a while. I told him that these things cannot wait and I need his help urgently. He comes to dad's station and says that he is helping but his shift is completed and he is not obligated to help. So, he wanted me to realize that he was doing me a favour. I then had to take him myself and waited outside the toilet for him to finish his work. I was with him for a while and then went home.

The next morning I was told he was recovering but then still had to be in the ICU for a few days. Dad wanted so desperately to get back home. I also wanted him back home but could not take him with the doctors scaring me so much with so many complications

The treatment in this ward was very bad. I had to scream at people to get every little thing done. If I questioned them about why they did not feed my dad or why some medicines were not given in time they would call the security and ask them to have me removed. I used to just sit outside and do my office work in between visiting him and then running around for medicines.

Every time a doctor would turn up and then there would be around 5 trainees around that doctor explaining the problem and that too right in front of the person who is ill.

I am not sure how this would have worked on my dad being told everyone that he is suffering from Cancer every day at least 2 times a day.

There was one nurse who was behaving like she was doing a favour looking after dad all throughout, she was showing all the anger she had elsewhere on dad and all the other patients. I told her that I would complain to the hospital authorities and then she started saying that she is doing everything she had to do. She changed the sheets, gave medicines, checked vitals etc and what more I needed. I told her that it might help being a little considerate and kind and she got so upset about it. More than dealing with the fact your loved one was ill you had to be on your toes with these people around who showed no signs of sympathy or empathy

I fought with her and left that evening. Dad's vitals were stabilizing and when I came in the next day I saw him a little more cheerful and stronger. However, I noticed that his hand was double the size of the original. I asked him what had happened and he said that the nurse had pricked his hand around 12 times and also stabbed it once as he was pulling off the monitor belt. He hated the monitor belt as it was hanging around his hand and irritated him so much.

I looked at the nurse in shock and asked her why she did that ? Dad had also said that she had not fed the lady in the opposite bed even though that lady had been asking for food for a really long while. The answers the nurse gave me was atrocious. She said that we should not pay too much heed to people who are in ICU, they are mentally retarded. When I walked in I noticed that she was talking to her mother on the mobile. I asked her- Can I ask you a question? Do you remember your mother's phone number? She said no. I told her. Ask my dad the number of the friend he spoke to six months back and he will give it to you. He never maintained a phone book. However, he would remember every single number by heart, I told her not to ever call my dad or for that matter any of the people admitted mentally retarded and treat them with respect. Maybe they were not in the right mind as they would usually be but that does not mean you treat them badly . This was a hospital not a mental asylum.

I felt so sad to see dad in pain and being someone who never bowed down to anyone till now in his life it sure must have been a physiological constraint what he was experiencing right now. He was not asked to do as per what everyone wanted him to. While to some extent it was important there could be better ways of communicating to him and getting him to adhere to it.

I had to get some kind of ointment to ensure that they apply it to get the swelling down. I was now scared to leave him alone at this semi-ICU as they were treating everyone very badly.

I went down to speak to the PRO on this matter and he gave me a long questionnaire which I filled out on his mobile. He said that the Director would call me in 15 minutes. It's been months when I am writing this and he has not bothered reaching out to me. Even when I have mentioned facts that would be shocking for him and would push anyone to take immediate actions to change things around the existing system.

It was good news the next day when they said that we could now take him to the general ward. I got him to a single ward which had a television and AC. AC was useless but I wanted him to have that privacy during his stay at the hospital and most importantly I wanted to ensure that he had a bathroom for himself and he could freely visit the bathroom. However, the bed placement for the caretaker was not comfortable as from where I would lie I could not see his face well. He had this habit of removing the oxygen pipe constantly and the Bipap machine. I could not monitor this from where I was. The oxygen pipe was definitely irritating. After checking we moved him from the big mask to the small nose plug in which was much more comfortable.

He barely slept in the night and I used to stay up with him the entire night. It was tough doing my day job and also being awake most of the time and able to manage calls during the day with total commitment, I did not expect my dad to understand but then he did. I remember one night when I had dozed off due to tiredness and got up suddenly to see him sitting on the chair without his gown. I quickly covered him up. He had the urgency to go to the toilet and did not want to wake me up. So, he had pulled himself up to go all by himself. I yelled at him for doing that and told him the reason I am at the hospital was for this and to ensure he lets me know when he needs any kind of help at all times. Maybe you can call it daughter's instinct but every time he used to wake up and sit very quietly I used to automatically wake up and be at his side. He is the best dad anyone can have.

This is what we had to manage for right now. The next day the lady at the next single room vacated and we moved there. Here I could have a clear view of dad. I used to lay awake the entire night watching and ensuring that I heard him when he needed me.

We stopped the hospital food as the quality and the taste was very bad. He was hardly eating anything they gave, I tried it once and it was really very bad. Dad was generally a picky eater. Being a hotelier, he was very choosy about the taste, while he was not particular about variety he would have two or three things and sometimes just even curd rice that he can gorge on. I got worried with the hospital food as I saw his diagnosis saying that his calcium was high but they had provided Curd for lunch and ended sending milk in the evening. When I asked the nutritionist, she said that they will give him as per the condition recommended by the nurses. When I checked with the nurse on what condition he was in she said that he had calcium deficiency and I asked her to recheck. I was clearly told that this was calcium high and potassium low. She checked and she apologized. That is when I decided to stop the hospital diet and food.

However, the taste of these items should be good for him to finish his food. So, I used to check with him what he wanted and order from Swiggy.

There was this one time when he asked for Kesari bath for dinner and I was super thrilled during this time. The best part was that he ate it all. I knew he was on the path of recovery, He was though very tired and weak, we had at this moment removed the Oxygen support and the Bipap which was absolutely another irritation off him

The only struggle was that he used to wake up sitting at nights as he used to have chest pain and trouble breathing. Whenever the doctors came on their rounds I kept telling them this and they said this is normal. Why do we need hospitals? Is it not the hospital that has to give us a remedy for problems?

I stopped going home to refresh and coming back and was almost on the same clothes for days together. His second wife would cone at around 12 and leave at 6. Most of the time he was very quiet absorbed in his world. Never uttering a word, sometime he became impossible and would not eat. This is the time I used to really get angry with him. Now I think I should have been more sensible to understand what he was going through instead of being impatient. He used to act a little illusion now but I could contribute it to the tablets he was taking. At one time he was so cranky that I told him I will leave to home and have this lady stay back. He did not like it at all. However, I wanted him to sleep and have some rest and he was not able to do that. I came home but was feeling so guilty. As soon as I got up in the morning

I went rushing to the hospital and was told that he did not sleep well and went to the toilet multiple times. This was basically a sensation and he was draining out all his energy trying to go to the toilet. He would never want to do in the huggies. At one time he was begging me to take him and I told him again that this was just a sensation. When we cleaned in the morning I realized that he indeed go to the toilet and I was feeling very bad about it. I did clean it up and explained to him that he could continue doing this and I will clean it up myself. I remember the nurse giving me gloves and I told her that he is my dad. I did not feel yucky about any of this but was glad that I was able to help dad out. I got him a commode seat and this made it a little easier for him to go the toilet. This remained a big problem during his suffering in the hospital. Many of his friends came and visited him in the hospital. At one time when they had visited and left and I was with him inside he suddenly started sweating and had breathing problem. I called to the nurse urgently and she attended to him as his pulse was increasing. I came crying out of the SICU not knowing what had happened. Later I went back to see that he had stabilized.

I was explaining to him that he should stop panicking and sometimes even in my Himalayan treks I would feel breathless and when I started breathing with slow breadths I would be fine, little did I understand what he was going through

Days passed by like this in the general ward. There was this beautiful sister called "Archana' who used to genuinely care for him.

She used to visit him and ensure he walks and then has his food. Literally forced him to eat. He was now becoming more impossible and one night I hit my head with a remote for him to go to sleep and take rest. He was so scared that I would get hurt and cried asking me not to do it. When I am writing this I still can't forget the way he folded his hands and asked me not to do it. I feel that was the craziest of things for me to have done and unable to forgive myself to put him through that stress. However, I was so worried that he was not eating and sleeping properly and in that process was affecting his health even badly and was nowhere getting closer to recovery.

I used to tell him that if he behaved this way I would call the nurse to come and tell him off. He would listen for a while and then start pulling out the oxygen mask or the syringe in his hand. I was so worried that they would come and poke in another one. Already his hand was now a bit blackish with so many needles and not only that. The pain that he had to go through was unthinkable

The next day the nurse was explaining to me that this is normal when so many medicines and the potassium low and calcium high would do to him are working on him. Also, once the levels are stabilized they will normalize and he will be back to normal. and I decided never to do anything like that again.

The doctor who was seeing him told me that he is in bad shape and only a miracle will save him. I believed in that miracle. However, he will never give me a solution to what he was suffering from. It was so robotic and mechanical and absolutely not one ounce of compassion. I told him to please help with the sleep issue and toilet problem. All this time he would be surrounded by trainees and keener on training them. These nurses would write down what doctors suggest and then not even bother to check on what that outcome was. I remember one junior doctor suggesting CBD oil and I asked him what is that given for and he said the senior doctor advised and he did not know what that did.

The nurses were still horrible. However, we had student nurses who were very kind. They used to come like clockwork and finish their tasks. I kept insisting that dad have a body bath as it will give him a sense of freshness. He used to not like it at all. I used to force him to try until the day I saw it happen in front of me. I saw that the body bath was via these wet body wipes. Even in that cold AC environment in ICU these members were given cold wet wipes and it was unbearable to watch. That was the time I refused to let anyone give dad a bath. Once in a while I myself got to wipe him with a hot towel which he was fine with.

I used to brush his teeth for him and he being a person with perfect oral hygiene now was never in a mood to brush his teeth. This showed the amount of pain he was going through and the part that he was not himself at all anymore.

The hours went into days and we were almost at a stage when we were ready to come back home. During this time, I met two beautiful sisters- Sister Catherine and Sister Celine. Such wonderful human beings. They came to the ward and said prayers for dad, had a good chat with him and left. This was a day before we were discharging him from the hospital. She asked me to come over to give me a glossary for dad and myself. I went over to the stipulated time the next day when we were getting ready for his discharge and got the glossary.

Although she refused the money I insisted and handed over some cash to the lady who gave me the glossary.

I came and gave that to dad. Dad was never spiritual except for that quick two-minute rush to the pooja room after bath every day. He will quickly mumble a prayer, look at all the gods around the house and get dressed. He used to like temples which were less crowded and just prayed . Not following the formalities that were tied around it.

I never knew what he was thinking when he had these visits for prayers for him. He was not even vocal about what he felt at these instances. He literally stopped talking altogether even though he was having a speech at this time.

He asked for Athirasam one day and I stepped out to get some for him, searching all the shops around. I used to love getting him whatever he wanted but never wanting to leave his side whilst I miss spending a moment with him. Thankfully I found some around and he just had one piece,

It did not matter as much as he even had one. He was watching TV for some time and posed for come pictures with the sisters when they came in to see him the next day. They told me to come and collect the recipe for a drink the next day, this was a powder of all millets that is supposed to give him strength. At this time, he did look much better than he was for a few days. He was wearing his favourite black sweater and looked very smart and handsome. While I showed him that picture he did take a deep look at it.

Also, at this time few strands of hair started coming back. He was extremely submissive listening to all that we used to say except put up a fight when he had used the diaper. I tried maximum to ensure he uses the bathroom and wash it for him.

Also, he used to get up to pass urine quite often, even though it was a sensation and he did not like the feel of wetting the diaper or the bed. It was so difficult to watch him struggle like this. The worst was when he used to be awake at night not able to sleep and I used to sit with him, coaxing him and motivating him to be strong. I used to keep saying that he has taught me to be strong and why is he scared now. Maybe I feel now I should have actually said that it is ok to be scared so that he could have easily shared what he actually felt and not hide it from me.

I got him back home in the afternoon and he was so happy to be back home. This time I was advised to only keep him on oxygen on and off and 5 litres was sufficient. They had still not advised Bipap even though they had used it in the hospital. Also, they had asked me to give him CBD oil and a few other medications but I did not see it on the discharge summary, When I called the doctor and also, I was told to continue with the medicines. I could not even ask why they did not mention it. This was the carelessness that scared me really badly. Not sure how they can be so bad on these things. It made me wonder if he really needed these tablets then.

They did write some tablets and when I say some- It was around 20 tablets in a day. He used to have it all so grudgingly and making him have these was such a task. I could imagine how I would have hated having these myself. When I saw saturation drop I would use the oxygen concentrator. When there were power cuts I would just leave it as the hospital themselves had not recommended the same.

The doctor called me outside and mentioned that it is now very difficult for him to survive further. He told me that he is sinking. I asked him to do whatever he takes to get him out and please be quick about it. I was surprised that he did not ask me to do a PET scan to see the state of the cancer till now. But I believed that they knew what they were doing and left it at lt.

During this time, I also wanted to try out the Shimoga cancer centre and one day packed the bag and left there to get the medicines. I was that desperate to try it out. There was a long queue for the medicine and they rarely saw the reports. I don't know how genuine this was at that moment. However, I met this guy who was in the queue who swore by this medicine. Apparently, his father had completed 8 chemos at HCG and the doctor had given up hope. He literally brought his dad carrying him back home. He mentioned that he was not even sure his father would be alive when he went back home with the medicines. But he has been giving him the medicine from thereon and his father recovered so well that he is able to do his own cooking as of now. This was really inspiring to me and I stood in the queue and got that medicine. It was a powder that you had to boil in water and drink it.

I came back and we prepared it for him the next day. Along with these 20 tablets he had this concoction also. He did not complain about this particularly but along with the 20 it was a big task to have this and I can totally understand how it was for him. As I had mentioned earlier he was someone who would not even take a tablet for fever stating that the tablet will reduce the immunity power. I started to notice that his saturation was dropping a bit gradually and it was almost like 85-90. He was also acting a little disillusioned and wrapping the blanket around his fingers. I was getting a little worried by now. His oxygen was maintained at 2-3 as instructed by the doctors. At this moment I was sleeping in his room itself as I wanted to ensure that I was available for anything that he wanted.

I realized that this lady was not taking care of him as much as I thought she would. He would always tell me this when he was alive but I would brush it off stating that there is nothing we can do at this moment and we need to live with it. He and I knew that we had absolutely no love for this woman but just tolerated her. She was always on the mobile and did not bother spending time with him or looking after his needs. She also used to keep making him feel like he was dirty when he was either smoking or drinking and tried to change his clothes which sometimes and very rarely stinked with sweat. She always kept washing stuff too even when he wanted it the most and forced him to eat what he did not like.

He used to not sleep at night at all. I had raised the bed as he would not be able to breathe if he laid down flat. He was so fidgety all through the night. I remember saying so many things to ensure that he ate and slept well. Some of this did hurt him but I thought at least he will try and eat well. Also, he was continuing to have this sensation of going to the toilet regularly but was too tired to go to the toilet. So, I brought him a can to use but he preferred the mug so kept one near the bed.

We at this moment called a nurse who used to come and visit him regularly and called him in the night to check what we could do. He asked us to increase the oxygen to 5 and we did that. Then his saturation level went up and stabilized but I was concerned about him being a little off in his actions. He refused to eat from the afternoon and I told him that I am leaving for Chennai the next day. I did mention that I am not getting any support either from his son or wife and I am trying to get him out of this but not able to. So, if I leave there will be no one to take care. I still feel bad saying that till date. I wanted him to just cooperate with me so that I can get him out of this once for all.

In the morning he was even worse and I got worried. The moment I will not forget is the fact that he bit my finger and nearly tears came out of my eyes. He felt so bad that he kissed my fingers. My heart just melted for him. Even today I cry when I write this. I now realized that maybe it will be a good idea to take him to the hospital as I was scared there could be an imbalance with the potassium or calcium like the last time.

While I was booking the cab, my brother offered to drive him to the hospital as he did not have college that day. It was more a matter of convenience for him. While I was not keen on it seemed better for dad so I agreed to it. At this stage dad was immobile and was not able to walk anymore. So, we had to carry him to the car. This was the first time he was getting in my brother's car as he was never asked even once after he purchased the car if he wanted to take him. Dad never wanted to get into his car.

But this time he was so lost that he did not even know what to say and just sat quiet. While time was the essence as he was off the oxygen concentrator my brother made sure he took the longer route as the shorter route damaged his car, I was just wondering how much my dad must be struggling to breathe. He also ensured he filled in petrol and this time I lost it and screamed at him. I wanted to get him to the hospital as quickly as possible. I told my brother that he could not be without oxygen for long and he was like he would not die if he did not have oxygen for 10 minutes and was so casual about it. Now when I think of the event that's happened later I think that he actually wanted him to die and was hoping that would happen on this trip.

I told him that his 15-minute hospital visits would not help him understand how crucial this was. He will only know when he spent time staying in the hospital there and spoke to the doctors or at least bothered to try and find out from me what was happening.

I had to shut up as I did not want dad to take any kind of tension on this. We reached the PH hospital and I immediately rushed to the OPD and told them I had dad outside and he was struggling to breathe

No one absolutely battered an eyelid. They were busy writing some records as usual and looked at me like I lost my mind. I had to literally scream at them to do something urgently as he was finding it difficult to breathe. Doctor - As usual they got a whole lot of trainees and then the doctor walked in. While I was requesting them not to do ICU they said if we did not then it would be life threatening as his CO2 levels were double to what it should be apparently, He explained that it was like he was standing next to a blowing car for the last three days and ICU was compulsory. They rushed him off to the ICU and I had to rush to get the admission done. They would not admit him till the time I made the payment. The guy at the payment counter was so slow in processing payments doing one thing at a time and was almost taking 15 minutes for one patient.

I told him that I needed to get my dad admitted to the ICU urgently . He still did not change anything on how he was doing things. Apparently, the cashier did not turn up for the day and they had put him in temporarily but that was a shoddy thing to do at a hospital without a backup person.

The person behind me literally told the cashier that they should finish mine first and everybody in the queue agreed and they hurried up mine really quick. They did a couple of tests throughout and then moved him to the ICU again. He was looking for me totally on where I was. The home nurse was asked to come to hospital as I thought she might be of help at the hospital but dad being moved to ICU is not going to help much as I asked her to leave and told them that once he is out I will have her come back.

They wheeled him over to the ICU and I was back to my waiting lounge at the ICU unit. This time was bad. They had put a Bipap and tied him to the bed as he was very wild and did not want to have the Bipap. I was surprised dad was behaving like this. However, it just went to show how frustrated he was and what terrible things must be going through his body. When I went to see him, he was sleeping with a Bipap and was signalling me to take him home.

I convinced him that he was getting treated and they were trying to pump the CO2 out, I was checking with the doctor on why this got filled in and he was saying that we should have kept the concentrator on, I told them that no one told us when we discharged him the last time. They did not have an answer to that at all. The entire drama of the ICU went on for another two days. Bringing medicines waiting outside and then meeting him during the visiting hours. He looked very very tired this time and they did so many blood tests and had pricked his hand again so many times

The next morning Dr, R came to see him and I was waiting outside to find out what this was about. They came out and took me to a room to discuss. I was all alone. As usual I was expecting them to tell me that he should be fine to leave in a couple of days and we can start treatment for him very quickly. I was not prepared to hear what they just mentioned.

R was like he had very less time and maybe a couple of days. It's better that he spends time with family than being in the ICU where he cannot meet any of us. I lost it and went into a trance. I had no idea what came over me but I remember having a blank. I remember this lady coming in and mentioning how she did not have anything written in her name and everything was in his children's name. I had absolutely no idea what the relevance was in this situation. I remember falling at the feet of the doctor asking him to save my dad. None of it worked and I threatened that I will kill myself if something happens to dad. The doctor threatened me that he would call the police if I kept going on like this. Then to my help came sister Catherine and she sat with me all throughout the time dad was made to come out of the ICU. During this time my brother had come in and the doctor had informed me that there was very much he could do anything (This was a month before he passed away). My brother then came to be and asked me to pay the bill for the room to have him shifted. I told him to do it himself as I was not in the right frame of mind to think about anything else. I went off to the lounge and called some of my friends for support, I will not mention their names here to keep their privacy,

Sister Catherine took me to the cafeteria to get me a drink as I had not eaten anything. During this time, I remember just eating one meal as he would not want me to be away from his eyesight at all and I had lost a lot of weight.

My brother was planning to move him to a three-sharing room and I totally refused. I wanted to give my dad some privacy and he did not deserve to be sitting in a room with so many people around. He went and inquired and came back stating that there was only a jubilee room and I asked him to go ahead, He was not happy about it as he had to pay. So, till now he had not spent a penny for dad. Even the home nurse incident was a bit of a joke for him. Not that he did not earn well but he was an absolute stingy person. Even when dad was alive he used to keep telling me how he was waiting for him to die so that he could take the property away. He had also mentioned what a great mistake he had made by bringing him back home after asking him to leave the house. There were times when dad would be finding it difficult to start the bike and be kicking it while this fellow passed by and he nor his wife would offer help. There were numerous such stories dad used to tell me about him when we were in the hospital and I realized how much dad kept all of this to himself to ensure that he does not create any negativity around the house.

A year back my brother was diagnosed with a cyst in his leg and I remember dad almost in tears as the doctors told us that it was so complicated due to his sugar problem that there was a possibility to amputate his leg. There were almost 6 hospitals that dad and I would have visited to ensure we got the right treatment for him. I was on a career break and it was the corona period at its peak. I was so worried about exposing dad to so many hospitals but he would just not listen and ensure that he comes to all the hospitals we went to. Due to the medicines my brother used to be depressed and act strange and dad used to do so many things to ensure that he got the right kind of treatment. I was never close to my brother, but during this time I ensured that I called all his friends to ask for help. We also went to his college to give him that moral support to speak to his superior to ask for a break from the college.

There was this one time when we had admitted him to the hospital after his leg surgery and we were sitting in the room for almost 9 hours. Dad did not even get up from the bedside. I told him that I will sit through and he can go and take a break. He said that if he wanted to go to the restroom he might not be comfortable telling me as female about it. He was someone who would always smoke at least once in an hour and the first time in my life I saw him not moving at all for almost 8 -9 hrs.

He used to come and keep dad awake by telling all his sad stories and dad would not complain at all. Now he did not even visit him to come and check on how he was doing for 10 minutes. There were times when he used to buy food and come in the evening and not even bother to come and check with dad if he wanted anything at all.

Later I remember him saying that when the niece came to see my dad I would lock the door and send her off saying that he was sleeping which was the truth. He complained that I was doing it purposefully. Only dad and I will know that he did not want to meet her at all.

Grudgingly he moved him to the jubilee room and went out to talk to his friends on the mobile.

We shifted dad to this room and he was looking much better than he was in the ICU. He was on oxygen concentrator and they had kept it around 9. He was also given the Bipap regularly, I was told that he would be on that for another three days, this was very painful for him and he did not like it at all. All my friends had now gathered up and were sitting with me.

On the other hand it was like a picnic for my brother and his family. She was laughing and talking to my niece and all I felt was the pain that my dad was going through. Somewhere my brother inquired and came to know that there was a room available in the normal single ward. I was fine in moving except that I had asked them to wait for just another day as he was already exhausted from moving from the ICU to this ward. He just did not agree. I also told him that I will pay for the hospital and he started screaming in front of my dad,

So, my brother is a lecturer but in no way did he have the decency to behave as one. He would just yell and scream and people like me who did not like that would just keep quiet .So when I had stepped out to grab something to eat they had already moved him out to a single room and my niece called me to tell me that they had moved him over. I went over to see him all wrapped up on the Bipap and I was feeling miserable for him. All my friends and these guys left, the words of the doctor left ringing in my ears and I would step out to cry and come back stronger to not show my dad that I was crying.

That night I remember holding his hand the entire night and not leaving his bedside even for a single minute. For some reason he started to always stroke my face with so much of love but he would have tears in his eyes, He was now not able to speak much. Just a few words now and then would come out.

But we remember spending so much time together talking about so many things. I did the talking most of the time. I told him how much I loved him and how he was the most wonderful dad of all times. He has made me so strong and gave me everything I needed and that I will always be so grateful to him. I told him that I am sorry sometimes to be a little impatient with him but the love for him never diminished. I am glad I told him all of these things now.

The next few days my friends ensured that they took care of me one after the other. one of them packed up a whole lot of clothes as I did not want to go home to get ready as I would miss time with dad.

They created a WhatsApp group to exchange messages on what steps need to be taken next.

Some of them brought me lunch and some of them stayed with me during the evenings. The days passed by like this. The best part is he took off the bibap when he was sleeping and thought he would die. I reassured him that it happens only in movies and he was not in that condition. In fact, the second day onwards, the nurses themselves took off the Bipap as he was maintaining the oxygen himself. This time however he was on oxygen forever and they had kept it to around 9 litres. He was so irritated with the mask. I literally begged them to give us a nose mask which was more comfortable for him.

He slept most of the time here and it was difficult to pass urine or go to the toilet. I assured him that I would ensure that he does not have to use the nappy and I will make him sit on the toilet stool. But every time we had to do that I had to get the help of the hospital staff as I could not lift him myself, I still did that. Then one time he had the sensation and I made him sit on the stool. But it became such a stress for him that I literally begged him to use the nappy so that it gets easier for him. Many times, when he used to not be able to pass the stool they used to manually induce this and when he did pass he used to be so relieved about the entire process.

This time around my niece started to come and see him regularly. Also, there was a kind of closeness she was trying to enforce upon him which dad did not like and mentioned that he was uncomfortable with this. I could not do anything but just ensure he was not out of my sight for long.

There was this one more time when he stole my heart. When his second wife and niece came to see him, he asked both if they had lunch and I was sitting there and he did not check. I was so hurt

I asked him why he did ask me and it hurt me. He just nodded his head and said I am there with him day and morning and he knows every minute of my move as he does not have to ask. I love him again and 10 times more. I gave him a big hug with tears in my eyes.

There were instances of misses again at the hospital. One night I noticed that his oxygen was totally empty and called the nurse. She came and filled it again. The nurses had been informed that he was in a critical stage but I did not expect them to give up on him. When I complained about anything they would say "You know his condition right" Yes, I knew it but that does not mean you let him to die right?

He was coming up well at this stage and I was told to take him home after a few days where he was looking to gain some energy. He was though on oxygen perpetually and this was not something that both of us were comfortable

able, Sister Catherine came and met him again and gave her blessings

I asked the doctor if we had to take a PET SCAN and he said we should. I arranged for this to be done one particular day and I took him this time to a private and different one in the hospital ambulance. We were completed and done in about an hour. I was running around the place holding dad, talking to the doctor and doing a lot of things and then they called me to pay the bill. I was in two minds on how to leave him alone with the attendants. But he looked at me silently and said they will manage you . So many of these instances made me realize that my dad's thought process was much deeper than what I thought it to be.

This PET scan was not very good either. The doctor said that there is nothing much that can be done now but will only work with a miracle. He then suggested an injection that they can try giving him and he said he will come to the hospital to give it on a Saturday – The day we had decided to take him home. I had arranged for the injection. This was the same one that M had recommended to be given to him. There was another doctor he had organized to give this injection. It was at least some kind of treatment that he was put to. This nurse Jy when putting together the discharge missed out so many medicines. I had to call up and check on why she had missed out and as usual she did not have an answer.

Also, I noticed that his heart rate had been high for a while. I kept calling them when it was going up and they said that the doctor is on her way to see and never made it. I could see dad was struggling with chest pain. These moments really made me wonder as to what the real reason behind the hospitals. Isn't something they are supposed to look into and provide help on- Are these hospitals now built for training and filling up millions of records?

I wanted to know how they knew that the CO2 level had dropped as I did not see them doing that particular test again. The doctor said he would know the symptoms if it was still high . But I remember this same doctor checking dads forehead and telling all the trainees that he had a fever and asking the nurse to give a DOLO. Dad was warm with all the blankets covered up and I asked the nurse to wait for some time and then check the temperature and later administer the tablet. When she checked later the temperature was normal. I did not want to infuse many more tablets into his system unnecessarily.

My friends ensured that they called up and did not leave my side at all. This time when I took him home I ensured that I had made a mini hospital set up at home as I did not want him to fall sick and come back to the hospital. I got him a reclining bed so he could breathe when fully down, and got him an air bed to give him the comfort to sleep.

I had also arranged a 10-litre oxygen and replaced the 5 litres. I called the power back up person and spoke about getting a backup. However, I wanted to get him home and then organize it. IT was a really bad decision. I got him back at home in the night as I did not want to see him getting down from an ambulance. This time around I also got the Bipap to ensure that the CO2 level is monitored regularly.

This time however he just refused the Bipap and almost begged me not to give him. I held it on for a while and not strapped it to make it comfortable but then he would not use it for more than 5 minutes. I just did not know how to handle this. He would also not sleep and kept telling me that he wanted to pass urine and I would tell him that he has a canister and he should pass it in here . He would just shake his head. After sometime It was good that he got used to this canister as it stopped his multiple trips to the toilet.

He also had the sensation of going to the toilet but he did not get anything as he was not eating well at all. We at this moment got the nurse and she was kind but had no clue on how the nursing was to be done in terms of medical work.

He ate when she told him to and actually his appetite increased. This time he stopped completely taking the medicine from Shimoga also. I was totally stressed out and seemed to be taking a toll on me as well as on him. However, I was very keen on ensuring that I get him out of this. The 10-litre oxygen guy had given me an oxygen cylinder for emergencies till I purchased the backup which I was planning to do in a day or two.

In the afternoon the next day there was a power cut and my heart stopped. I had to immediately get him onto the oxygen as I did not want a repeat of the CO_2 build up and him going back to the ICU again. I immediately went to switch on the manual cylinder he had provided me and it did not work. I tried so much and nothing happened. It was almost 5 minutes and I could see the discomfort building up with dad. I then went up to my tenant above and asked her if I could use her backup and switch on the concentrator. The challenge is how would we take dad on top. In the meantime, I called the concentrator person (Name) and he said there is absolutely no guarantee he would give us the cylinder and it would take another hour to get us a backup.

Did not look like he was bothered much and wanted to wash his hands off the whole process.

The power capacity of the tenants backup did not help. It was at a lower capacity. It was like I was in a trance and went mad with pressure.

I then jumped over to the neighbour's house and asked them if we could fix the concentrator there. It did not work either and not he was really struggling to breathe. With the help of my tenant we managed to get an ambulance with the concentrator in it.

He was quite surprised to see that we needed the ambulance only for the oxygen concentrator. Dad was shifted to the concentrator and he ate really well now. This was a good sign that all was well. I do remember my brother and sister in law coming and passing dad in the ambulance without even a blink of an eyelid, they did not even come inside to see what was happening. At this time I had got the backup person to come and set up the backup and the electricity was also restored. This was not a good day at all.

We then had the ambulance go back and got dad shifted back to the room. At least this time I was happy that we did not leave him without oxygen for a long time. It must have taken me 20 minutes to set up the ambulance completely.

Due to this lapse I thought I would try and use the Bipap for a while but he completely refused to use it. I just sent a silent prayer to god to ensure that all was well and nothing got messed up due to this delay.

In the meantime, the swelling in his hand had not gone away and I did not want to take him to the hospital again.

It was not painful but knowing dad even if it was I don't think he would say that it hurt him. So, I checked on the net and arranged for a doctor to visit him home to see the swelling. A team of a doctor and an admin person along with a nurse came along and attended to his hand. They applied a layer of some gooey stuff, the same that was done in the hospital and bandaged it, they charged an exorbitant amount for that. The swelling was mainly due to the fact that the nurses had stabbed it multiple times to ensure they get a vein

The doctor looked at the report and said that it did not look very nice. I told him that he was having issues on the toilet also. They provided a tablet for that and left,

During this time, I had asked his help in putting the Bipap in a comfortable way so that dad will at least use it for some time. He refused completely and I was shocked to see the hospital had charged me Rs. 500 for this additional 5 minutes where he was trying to fix the Bipap. I already knew how this had to be done. However, I only took his help as I thought there could be a much more comfortable way of doing this. This is what the hospitals does and we don't have choice but accept it,

They left and dad ate little and slept. His meals now consisted more or less of liquid stuff and he would once in a while ask for some curd rice or bun. He loved bun and coffee at this moment, He also like bananas but we had to stop non – veg (He anyways) did not eat this either ways

Now most of the time he had Manna and a protein drink called Ensure. As soon as he got up I used to fix him at around 4 in the morning. He was hungry nowadays which I always saw as a good sign. He also ate a bit of apples

. It was so sad to see him manage his meals in this way when he used to be so particular about what he ate. This lady slept on the hall because she was getting disturbed, all though she would hear our voices she would be busy with browsing on the mobile but never step in to see if we needed any help at all.

He was really upset by the fact that he could not go to the toilet. He would get up with the urge and sit down near the bed but nothing would happen and he would be frustrated.

The last Non-veg meal he had was when his friends had come down to the hospital and he asked for Biryani to be ordered for everyone. I had to smash the biriyani so that it was easier for him to swallow. He must have had just a few bites and stopped eating. I was thinking at this time maybe he was hiding the fact that it was difficult for him to swallow the food.

When the doctor was at home we noticed a note on the concentrator which said" Low O2 "and then it would automatically switch off. The doctor said that is coming because the concentrator is kept in a very bad closed environment. This will be a problem for the night. I searched the net and saw that they asked to clean the filter when such a message came up. So, I did all of that in the night but still the message just kept coming and switched off. I could not even reach out to the guy for any help as it was the middle of the night. My job was only to keep switching it off and on the entire night to ensure that dad did not lose out his power off the oxygen.

During the time I was still sleeping in dad's bedroom I realized how dingy it was. There was absolutely no circulation of air at all. So now I opened up a few windows also. They were all so messed up. I was wondering what kind of house this lady was keeping and also felt a little guilt from my end for not noticing this earlier when dad was healthy.

I sent a message to the guy at around 4 in the morning and he responded by 4:10. I told him and rather screamed at him for putting my dad's life at risk. He said he will make it to the house with a replacement concentrator but it would take about an hour. I did not have a choice but to wait

He then came over and agreed that his concentrator was at fault – So he had actually ended up giving me a manual oxygen cylinder and also a faulty oxygen concentrator. He replaced it with two five litres and connected both along with the backup that was installed now. That also was kind of dripping. The guy came over and said that there was no problem with the backup but the phase of electricity flowing through was not enough to support the back up. This was another problem now, I called the electricity board and they came in twice to check and said it is not their problem. I was literally begging them to do something as it was the matter of my dad's life ,

The guy who came was so insensitive to the whole thing and just went off saying there was nothing he could do and not call him unnecessarily. I then called our local electrician and asked him to see if he can directly give a connection to the Backup and he agreed to do it, this will avoid any kind of fluctuation to the backup

He gave me a huge amount to pay and I agreed again. He was quite shocked to see dad in the fashion he was a regular to our house and seen dad in better form earlier. He worked very quickly to get the work done and we did some external wiring and got it fixed. I now thought my problem was fixed and charged the backup completely. I was told that it will withstand almost 5 hours without electricity and I was sure that we might not have a power cut more than this and this was ample time to create a backup plan even if the power cut extended to about 3 hrs. Just as planned there was a power cut at around 2 p. m and I called the electricity board to find out when it would be back. They confirmed that some work was being done at the pole and it would take about an hour. This was not very reassuring, I knew well that if there was pole work then it was a long procedure and not to trust what these people say especially as it involved my dad.

I asked them where the work was being done and went to that place. There indeed was some heavy work being done, these people were all having coffee. I asked them how long it would take and they told me 30 minutes which again was something I did not trust. They were having a relaxed time and just chit chatting. I don't blame them. I don't think it was their problem to cater to such emergencies.

I went up to the lead and spoke to him. I mentioned to him that I had my dad on oxygen and the power would just last for another three hours and if the power would not be back by then it would be crucial for dad.

I was reassured that it would be back by one hour. I went back home waited for another hour and then called up electricity board again They said that work was still ongoing and it would take about another one hour, Now I started to worry, although there was no issue at the pole but they were changing the phase at the poles and I knew their commitment of time was nothing that can be trusted upon

I went up to the chief engineer and explained the problem to them. The people were doing the work but I had very little buffer time now. I just had another hour left for the backup to go off. If by god's grace it extended then good else it would be trouble. I stood right there with the engineer and kept requesting him . He did mention to the other guys to finish fast as there was a patient involved which was actually very kind to him .

They finished the work with just 15 min to go and he said he will go to the main place and switch on the mains. I pleaded with him to do it asap and he said it would hardly take him two minutes and asked me to go back home. I did and the power had not come. Now I started looking for backup plans, but in about 5 minutes to my relief the power was on.

During these days the nurse was there. Initially she was very alert and careful but this lady in the house kept talking stories with her and gossiping right in front of dad not even allowing him to sleep.

He was now getting irritated with her as she was starting to get a little bossy. There was one time he almost spat the food back at her. Although I did feel bad she said not to bother, she also helped in cleaning up if he wanted to go to the toilet. This lady kept referring to dad as "Do you look after people like this" as if dad was an outcaste and I used to keep telling her to watch out what to say and what not to even if he was asleep.

She used to also show his diaper to people when they came to see him and I used to close it up. Now the 20 tablets were not needed, I did not know how these doctors wrote medicines. They wrote at their whims and fancifies I suppose.

I also stopped giving the Shimoga medicine as dad hated it and it was very sour. The lady had come for about just three days. Suddenly in the morning he stopped eating completely, I blackmailed him saying that I have informed all his friends that he is not eating something again that I feel bad doing even till day. His friends starting coming in one by one to tell him to eat.

I had also agreed at this time that once he gets fine I will get married to whomever he selects and also had told him that we will sell off that property that I had purchased in Chennai. He was not at all happy with that and was always trying to convince me to sell it off, the plan was to sell it and buy a flat before he fell ill. I wanted him to select the house as it has always been him standing in the forefront for any big purchase in my life, He has been the deciding factor of any of this, now dad's friend talked to him about how he has to get better and then get ready for my wedding, they wanted to fix it in January so he has a month to recover.

Dad just nodded his head, He still did not get to smile and at this moment again could not speak well at all.

The last time he smiled was when this same friend had come to see him in the hospital and told him to come home quickly as the marriage had to be completed. He smiled and asked the friend: You guys have already decided to pack me up, haven't you ?

This whole day he did not eat anything at all. Suddenly he was pissed off about something. I told him I am sorry to have told his friend and he said it was not anything about that, He just did not express how he was feeling at all. I had told him the evening earlier that I will get back to Chennai if he was refusing to eat and I apologized for doing that too. I promised him that I will not go anywhere leaving him and be with him 24/7.

As evening came in I kept asking him if he was fine and then asked if he wanted to go to the hospital

He actually shook his head and said yes. That made me realize that he must be really struggling with something as he would have never said yes. But he said he wanted to go to Bowring and I agreed. I called up multiple hospitals to find out if they had an OPD and if they would take a cancer patient. Many did not have and some did not even respond. While some of them agreed when I mentioned he was already in treatment for cancer they refused to take him in. Finally, we decided on taking him to Bowring. However, I realized that in a government hospital for his condition he might not get treated well and then decided to call Dr R. I asked him if I can get him to the hospital where he was practising – B and he said that it was not a good idea and it would be very expensive -. I told him that it was fine and I did not want to take him to Ph again. While he said that Ph was good I thought I saw worse and then convinced him that I will get him to B and took him there.

He called up the hospital and told them to expect dad. However, when we went there the doctor had to call him and consult him as to what needs to be done. He was kind enough to book us on a normal ward cost.

I did not want to take him to Ph again at all and put him through torture again at the hands of those trainee nurses. I called in the ambulance we used for getting him back home from Ph. This bunch of people were very helpful. It was pouring very badly and the ambulance struggled to get into my small street but somehow, he came in. We covered dad with an umbrella and took him to the ambulance. When this lady asked my brother to join he literally said why was he needed when we were going. He also had the audacity to tell her why we were still struggling to save him when the doctor had asked us to give up.

Appa always had trouble sleeping down in the ambulance as he had difficulty breathing. Hence, he would sit up and even now I still remember his head bobbing up and down as the ambulance as we rushed past the traffic and it was terrible to see him struggle with his breathing.

Once we reached the hospital they took him immediately to the OPD and examined him and he was indeed in bad shape. He would never say he was struggling ever and it was so difficult to accept that something was wrong with him.

We went there and when I went to the billing counter I was just signing the form as they said they would have to admit him to the ICU and his CO_2 level was so high that I collapsed. I woke up in another room and was upset that I could not see my dad being taken into the ICU. The hospital convinced me that I should take some rest as my BP had gone very low and they would allow me to see him in the ICU later. I knew dad would be looking out for me. He was always looking out for me and if he did not see me he got very panicky

I did gain some energy and went looking up for him on the third floor. This lady was suddenly very caring towards me and I did not like it a bit. She who used to speak so well to my brother now behind his back started cursing about him that he did not come.

She was an ultimate hypocrite and I did not even trust her one bit.

I then went and saw him in the ICU. I must say I was very happy when I saw the set up. It was much quieter and more peaceful and looked more appealing for a person admitted. However, I was not very happy to see dad strapped to so many machines and pipes. It was a horrible sight and I struggled to even pass that memory today when I wrote this. I went out and wept like crazy, this lady had already gone to sleep and I wondered how she did not even bother wanting to know how he was in the ICU, I do remember thinking if this was my mother she would have sat outside the ICU no matter what rules the hospital had and this lady was happily sleeping in bed with no worry and checking on WhatsApp on her mobile. I felt sad that dad had to put up with someone like this and I did not help him when he had mentioned about how bad she was earlier. I used to see her taking care of his needs and was surprised when he complained but now I see he was right in saying she only did that when I was in Bangalore. I also remember that she never used to call me when I was in the earlier hospitals to check if he was doing fine. It looked like she was doing the hospital visits as a formality.

No wonder he liked it when I was in Bangalore at this time he was being taken care of and the fact that I was always with hm to love him and treat him on top priority

The visiting hrs was only in the evening and I went to the ICU to check on how he was doing and they told me not all that great, He was still having breathing difficulty and was on the pipes along with the BiPap. The entire day I sat in the hospital just waiting to hear news. This lady had left early morning and she said she will come back later that day,

This hospital was very far from home. Almost a two-hr drive and a 1. 3 if we take the metro and change two trains. So, I could not even step out from the hospital as there was nothing to do for me to do outside the hospital

It was a nerve wrecking moment not knowing what was happening inside. Then the doctors who were on duty came over to speak to me and said that he was in a really bad shape and this kind of breathing trouble was something that would be common due to the bad condition of his cancer. I cried as I could not do anything . They told me that it's better we do not do anything more else it will just put him in more pain, I listened to them and was so handicapped to do anything else.

He was on the bed looking so weak but much better than what he did the previous day, However the tubes were still there and had to be given oxygen. They had reduced the pressure to 4 which I thought was good news. They did mention that the CO2 was still high. They wanted to take him out for a brain scan and had removed the Oxygen support to see if he can sustain the visit to the brain scan. It was 15 minutes and he was doing fine. I went out and waited outside the scan centre to get one look of him. They had still not taken him for the brain scan as yet. I was not able to understand if this was just a normal delay or if he was not able to sustain without oxygen. I went up to the scan place again multiple times to check if they had got my dad and they had not. One thing I noticed here was that the people were actually friendly and spoke to you at least politely when asked about some queries.

I remember when in Ph's we were taking him home I kept asking how we can check if the Co2 levels came down and the doctor told me that with his symptoms they will be able to judge. I did not think very highly of this as it was this same doctor who came and checked him and said he had a fever by looking at him and asking to give him a tablet. He was already on so many tablets so I requested the nurse to actually first check the temperature and then decide to give him a tablet.

When checked he had no fever. Till date I am still not clear on what basis they said he was fine on CO2 levels. They just increased the Oxygen level to 9 and sent him home. Now I see that it had gone up higher and the doctor just blankly told me that this is normal

What I could not understand is then did they just wait for him to pass away? Why then did Monco take his case and then was handed off by telling me that it was his diet and immunity that was a problem. His immunity was good when we started.

Anyway, we had no other choice than just wait and listen to them tell us to wait. I waited in the lounge and then my lawyer uncle came in and saw him. However, this time when we saw him he was looking much better than before but still weak.

Lawyer uncle went and spoke to him and he was looking at him but could not speak. He stayed with me till the evening and then left

I was all alone in the waiting lounge. At this time my brother had come with family and apparently, they told the security they wanted to see dad and he did not allow them inside, the security told me later that my brother told him that his younger granddaughter has come to Bangalore and since dad was going to die it would be good to see him for one last time. Did he just assume that we will let him die like this, and if he was so sure how come he did not even come and visit him at the hospital? Some questions to which I did not have answers- But neither did I have time to sit and think about it. I made up my mind to completely cut off my ties with him from a very long time off. I do believe in Karma and I am definitely waiting to the way it is going to work

But I took permission from the doctor and showed my dad to my lawyer uncle. All you had to do was request and not throw your weight around I suppose. Some things a few people do not understand. After coming out this time I was a little more relieved that he was at least able to recognize people.

When uncle left I was sitting all alone and so worried. At around 2 in the morning I got a call from the ICU and went running. The doctor called me inside and said that dad was in bad shape and was gasping for breath . She told me that this kind of breathing was not good and he might be in a position to die any moment. She said it was her duty to get a document signed off from me not to take any drastic steps. I keep wondering how particular these doctors are then being sensitive to what is happening to the family of the person in the hospital.

I went out and went to the chapel and prayed. I had his shawl around me and I just kept holding that and crying.

All I wanted was just him to get out of this misery. If he had limited time then fine. But I was asking God not to let him suffer in this manner.

It dawned and I went up to see if I could get any information on how he was doing. I saw the same doctor and she told me that he was much better now but still under observation. I went back to waiting at the lounge.

When the time for visiting came I went in again and was so happy to actually see all the masks out from his face and he was actually sitting up and able to recognize me. They had decided not to take the brain scan as he was normal at this moment. He asked for coffee and I was super thrilled. I really thought this was a miracle that was worked upon due to my prayers. I literally had the prayers on my headphones and had gone to sleep. He smiled at me and I asked the nurse if I could get him coffee. She had agreed and said she will arrange for the same.

I hovered around talking to him and chatting about how I am sitting out only and how the children had come to see him. He was asking for his glasses which I gave him and he was showing off to the nurses who told him that he looked very handsome.

He wanted to know where everyone was and then this lady walked in to see him. I left them talking for some time and went back to the waiting room. I however wanted to spend so much more time with him and actually see after a long time .

He was also started to talk and the words were coming out easily. He spoke about wanting to go home and I told him that at this time I am not taking him home. I made him understand that how every time I had taken him home on earlier instances he felt sick and I had to get him back to the hospital. My idea was to get him to Chennai to any beautiful place in ECR and try and help him gain back his strength and then put him on the treatment

This time I was planning to take him to a care home where they will work on getting him back to health and then put him on treatment.

During my stay there, I was googling a few places and came across a few in Koramangala. I knew he would not immediately agree to be taken out of Bangalore. So, I looked up this one place and was contemplating the location. I had called up a few and got the rates and other details from them. I really wanted a place where there are some Greenery and he will be able to breathe fresh air and try to get some routine and be able to gain back his appetite through the treatment that they will provide. At one time I got a call from this one person who said I had sent him an inquiry . I did tell him that I was browsing through a few places and looked around for some airy spaces. He mentioned that his place fitted the bill and it would be good to get dad out there, While I spoke to him and said I will decide about it he mentioned that he would come the next day and speak to the doctor whom he knows and will also see dad and go.

While I was impressed with the effort he was taking to come and see him I was a little wary on whether this will be the right place for him and wanted to check before I met this person. He told me he was a doctor in Nimhans and then left to start this program to rehabilitate cancer patients. That day dad actually spoke well and I explained to him that I will be taking him to this place. He did request saying that he wanted to go home. I told him that if we go home we do not know what is happening and keep coming back to the hospital and I really did not want to do that till he was able to walk by himself. He agreed and he did get a little scared when I got him here last time as he had difficulty breathing.

The doctor from Nihmans came in the next day but did not know my doctor as he had mentioned he knew. He spoke to dad and told me that he should be able to get him back to health and he did not look as bad as he thought he would. Dad was also looking convinced with this gentleman and was happy to be moved. We then went to meet R at his cabin.

I was seeing his cabin for the first time with a lot of Godly pictures around and a lovely fragrance which I mentioned to the doctor. We spoke about dads health and he was saying that he is still figuring out how best he can try and save him from this. He came up to meet dad and told dad that we will be going to this home and get healthy and he will take him back to continue the treatment for his cancer later. The priority now was for him to get better to be able to sustain further treatment that had to be administered to him.

Dad just nodded and said OK. I really wanted dad to be fine in this decision. He has always been a man of his own words, He would never at any point listen to anyone else or go by anyone else's opinion unless he strongly believed it. This strapped to bed was not something he was quite enjoying and I was thinking how this was affecting him psychologically more than physically.

The man who was ruling his world and not dependent on anyone is now unable to walk even a short distance did leave him more handicapped in the mind than his body and it tore me apart to think that he was going through this.

There were multiple times that he was undressed in front of the doctors and nurses and sometimes people who came to see him. Whenever this happened I could see him cringe and make sure that his modesty was saved. I would also turn the other side if I felt that he was uncomfortable with me standing there. During times when I had to clean him up after using the toilet I could sense he was uncomfortable and I would tell him that this was perfectly fine. Did he not do it when I was a little baby?

The doctor then gave the green signal to let daddy go home. The hospital was quite surprised as they usually move a person from ICU to the general ward before allowing them to go home and here they were moving him directly out of the hospital

The Ksh home sent an ambulance and a nurse along with the Van and an admin person. One look at the nurse and I was wondering if I was taking the right decision. It was too late now. I had requested two things to the doctor at the Nimhan's that the room should have good air circulation and a private room and also a TV so that he is distracted with some form of entertainment.

They took us to the home which was situated in a busy residential area. The doctor at B set him at 4 oxygen levels which was a good sign as they had put him on 10 when he left PH the last time. I got to know later that keeping him on high Oxygen was not helping much and it should not be the case. The place where they had to take him was on the second floor and the lift was not working. I had no clue how they were to take dad on a wheelchair to the second floor along with the oxygen cylinder.

One more thing I noticed with anyone handling a person from a wheelchair or bed and trying to lift them actually never bothered to check on how the person felt when he was being lifted. They would just hold the hands or chest and lift him without even asking if they experienced any pain holding him there and I used to always see dads face at these moments to see if he was doing fine or position had to be changed. 8 out of 10 times he was not ok as they kept their hand to lift him at a sensitive spot on his lungs.

They all carried him to the second floor to a room which was unbelievable. Till the end I did not believe that this is where they were going to keep him and not at all what I was promised by that doctor. Firstly, it was not a single room. There was another person at the other place who was coughing so badly all throughout the day and night. They barely had a screen covering both of them and the place was stinking. The other person was also bedridden and could not move around. We were promised one person who will look after two people . There was absolutely no greenery around the room. It was worse than keeping him at home. I thought let me wait till morning as it was already around 9 pm and then take a call on what needs to be done.

There was this one guy who was looking after both and he was complaining all the time how he was overworked and had no one to replace his duty. I kept listening to him for the sake of being polite but I really did not want this kind of negativity at this moment. The surprising part was as soon as dad entered the room he uttered the word "Godown" and it hurt me really bad to have got dad here,

It should have been a good idea for me to come down first and see the place and then decide whether to get him here or not. This was a lesson I learnt.

I am sure if I had seen this place first I would not have got him down here at all. The other old man was also a cancer patient and was all alone, He kept talking to himself the whole night and it was disturbing dads sleep, I told the attender and was shocked when he actually went and slapped the old man. I told him that was not a right thing to do at all but he was least bothered about it.

We had to put up with it at this moment as there was nothing I could do about it. Even if dad was mobile I would have immediately taken a cab and moved him far away from this place. His condition and the fact that every time I moved him around he just kept quiet and came along gave me the thought that he trusted me so much on doing what was right for him and this time I knew I had failed him miserably. They had fixed the monitor with the thumb machine which dad hated. I realized that they fixed it only to maintain the oxygen reading so I asked them to give me an oximeter instead. At this moment he was almost at one litre and I kept wondering how he was maintaining saturation at almost 95 – 98 with just one litre when PH had kept it at 9. We just had to blindly go with the advice given to us. That night I was sleepless again as I saw the oxygen level dropping and then suddenly noticed that the oxygen machine was not working at all. They had mentioned that it was a centralized system and oxygen flowed from that centralized place but then when I touched the tube there was no air coming out of it at all. I went down to the reception and complained about it

He immediately informed the security and they were checking. In the meantime, they shifted the oxygen to the physical oxygen tank that was kept there when they brought him upwards, He was now breathing ok and they got it sorted . I was now so scared if this happens again when I am asleep then what to do. The attender was someone that I could not trust. I was on all alert now and vigilant throughout the night. It was almost around four months since I slept for more than two hours a day. Even when that lady came in she was not concerned how his reading was or how to look after him. She would be fidgeting the mobile or talking to the nurses and distracting even their work. She was always gossiping .

While I was going through his predicament was even worse. He rarely slept and also had to sleep with all the propped pillows as now this had become a habit for him.

Morning the attender was looking after that other person who needed a lot of attention and left dad who was not wanting any kind of bath or brushing, I insisted that he get it done as it will give him a feel of freshness and he agreed to do it, He was not taking too keenly to this place. He was talking a bit but very less. It was magical however that I was the only one able to understand what he was saying. After getting him ready myself with a hot towel bath and brushing his teeth I started to monitor all the medicines the hospital had given. The nurses had not even administered a single one at this moment, nor did they provide him the nebulizer that was prescribed. They all looked like novices who had no idea on nursing but were trained to do certain monotonous tasks and activities. But definitely not trained to handle any kind of emergencies or need which was surprising to the kind of place they were stationed at as you would expect only very critical and dependent people to come in here. The need of the hour would be emergencies.

Now suddenly dad's voice went down and I asked him what happened. He was like it was going and coming and he was not sure why.

I told him not to worry, they did keep a Bipap but was told there is no need to provide that to him now. The nurses were horrible and the service was pathetic. Also had to keep listening to the attender cribbing about how bad his work was at this place and how they did not pay him well. Sometimes I saw him do like a 24/7 shift and was not sure how alert he could have been if he continued in this manner. There was food provided on the terrace but it was so bad. So, I went out and ate and come. I had to quickly rush out when this lady was there as I did not trust her to look after him well. Dad was still on the urine catheter and B had actually fitted him with a food pipe when he was in ICU. We were not sure when to take it off. Dad was saying that he was actually comfortable taking food through the mouth and the food pipe was irritating him.

I found the dietician, a young girl extremely helpful and the only best part of this place. She told me that we should keep him on the tube for a longer time and she used to keep sending the food on time. When it did not come I used to call her and she did say it was the attenders responsibility who was not bothered at all and expected me to take care of all this which I generally did.

She told me that if they started giving him food orally at this moment there are chances of it getting stuck in his throat and might affect his breathing. I left it to her as she was one person who looked like she knew what she was talking about. But she did promise me saying that after two days she will try and give him something very light on the solid front and see how that will settle with him before taking a call to go ahead with removing the pipe. I knew dad was not tasting anything right now. It was all these fluids going directly through the pipe. He was feeling bad and I was equally depressed about it. The only good thing was that some form of nutrition was being fed to him. I did occasionally give him very tiny bits of chocolate to get some taste into the mouth. He liked it.

The purpose of coming here was that I got involved in this lesson and actually got to spend some quality time with dad which was not happening. I was always running around telling them to do their job and calling them to fix something or the other that was amiss. He was not happy being told off and I kept interfering on what medicines to give him. Dad really wanted to go home and I started finding places in ECR where I could take him off.

Many times, I have seen tears in his eyes and he used to touch my cheeks and I used to ask him why he was crying. He never said anything. I felt he was slowly losing hope and that is the stage I did want him to go to . I also sensed that he did not tell me all the problems he was facing as he did not want me to get worried and also not waste money on him. On finances I was struggling now. I had to keep shelling out my money and had no other support coming in. This part I was ready to go to any extent. I would sell all I have if it came to that. But I knew my dad would not want me to do that. He used to always have me save my money for a brighter tomorrow.

My brother and his family came to see him once and voiced their dissatisfaction at this place. He asked him if he wanted him to get any juice and my dad nodded "Yes" and I knew why. But my brother never bothered getting him anything.

A few days back in the other hospital my brother's friend had visited dad and, on the way, picked up pomegranate juice which was a favourite of dads. My dad would never ask or take anything like that even from his very own close friends. However, since he had already purchased it he drank it all. The next day when my brother asked him if he needed juice he said no. So, my brother very sarcastically said that "Only if my friend gives you will drink right"? I only knew how much my dad was hurt at this remark. That is why when he asked now without any choice he just nodded his head.

Till now he has not been vocal at all about all the pain he has been going through. He was a kind of person who would never want to ask for help, even till date he has never asked me to change anything on my work to focus on him. Even this one time when I had an important call and at the same time had to take him to the ear clinic he said patiently waiting for my call to get over to get back home. Now when I think of it I feel so guilty. I should have just dropped everything and just been with him at all times.

Never a cribber or a complainant.

There was a speech therapist who was assigned to come in twice a week 30 minutes a day. I was not sure what she was going to achieve with this time slot. I saw her working with the other gentlemen in the room and did not have him reach anywhere.

There was also a Physio who popped up and asked dad to move his legs and hands around, Dad was so tired he just did not cooperate , She said she will come back in the evening and never turned up after that. I felt they were applying one rule to everyone and not going about reading and acting upon specifics about each case.

He was currently at oxygen level at 1 litre and the main doctor came over and said it would be safe to take him off the oxygen and then did that, He however went down to 80 and got breathless. I told the doctor who then immediately got the oxygen back. It all looked like a trial and error that was being managed at this place, they had no idea what was happening. I was still in the lookout of changing him to another room which was what I had asked for earlier and one was empty, for some strange reason they refused to move him out to that place. I actually saw a new patient being moved there and when I asked the administration , I was given a vague answer which I was not satisfied with .

They then showed me a room with a lot of equipment with the window facing some construction work. They said they will remove the equipment and clean up the room. While I appreciated them doing this I was not sure how the view would look for my dad. He was already getting frustrated with this place, I knew all he wanted was to go home, I was so scared to take him home if in case something goes wrong again and I had to get him back,

The room smelled of oils and they assured me that they will clean it and give a TV. While they managed to remove the equipment the smell still remained and when I saw the room in the morning it was a disaster- There was a construction happening next door and the window was prone to all that noise coming from there, it was terrible moving him from one room to another and I did not want to shift him again. I had to move my bed closer to the window so that he does not get to see this sight a lot. It was all cramped up. We also got one attender for him looking after him 24/7.

This was supposed to be a trained nurse but did not have any of the looks of it. The entire team looked like it was put together as an experiment. Dad did not trust this guy at all for some strange reason. He used to keep pointing to him and making faces for me to stop talking to him every time I asked him something.

I had to constantly watch over him in case he was pulling off the oxygen mask or if he was going through any pain. He rarely would wake me if I slept and just sat all quiet and alone not telling what was happening with him. Hence, I would just sit and chat with him making him feel comfortable and hoping that he does not feel alone.

He was not in a good space. He was not able to speak, was very tired and could not eat properly due to which the tube was attached. Due to only fluid intake he was also not able to go to the toilet and he used to just get the sensation and irritation that he was not able to pass freely. At some point on this matter I thought he had accepted this but at times he insisted that he stepped out of bed to go to the toilet. I also brought him a bed pan but to no avail.

Also, he was always sleeping while sitting up. As now when he kept his head down he was feeling breathless and hence preferred to sleep this way. I used to set up about six to seven pillows for him but he used to always hang his head down. Once the doctor told him when his breathing became difficult to sit upright to ease the breathing- But no one tried to understand what his problem was when and the reason as to why he was not able to do that.

I used to keep telling them that he was having heart problems , unable to sleep and not able to go to the toilet. No one looked into what needs to be done to solve for these. I saw this constant behaviour in all the places I had him admitted. I was just so helpless that I could not solve for these issues that he was complaining about.

When I was monitoring the oxygen the next day we moved him to the new place. I suddenly noticed that his saturation reading was going down. When I called them to check they took almost two hrs to come down and check what was happening. Then they realized that actually there was again no oxygen flow from the pipe they had installed. There was a cut off somewhere and they had to get the manually pre-set up. This was the second time it was happening and no one took responsibility to solve for this.

By this time dad's breathing became laborious and they said that they will have to take him to the hospital to put him on the ventilator or else another option was leave him as it is for now and see how he fares up. The ventilator was a painful process and was advised against it even when he was at B. The doctor had told me that that could leave him on bed support with no way of coming back and it would really be painful for him. He had the Bipap fixed and he was struggling to get the saturation back to normal.

I was in a dilemma now on what needs to be done. I really wanted him to be saved and then not regret that if we had not tried that out it could have actually saved him. However, at this moment I saw the saturation go up and wanted to wait. All this as the oxygen did not flow through the pipe and it was very disappointing that they had a system that worked so bad.

He finally was a little better and we removed the Bipap and had him on regular oxygen. They had put the Bipap so tight over his mouth that the food pipe had actually made a cut on his lips and I am sure that must have also been painful. When we got him back from Ph too the Bipap had made a nasty mark on his nose. He was so tired with all this drama in the night. Somehow after coming to this place he was barely able to sleep in peace even for a single day. I was also trying my best to see the most comfort I can give him and I was struggling with that,

At this moment I ensured he had a warm body rub and brushed his teeth to ensure he feels fresh.

His second wife came and saw him between 12 – 6 and went back. I did not mind being with him the entire time. I was just not getting the heart to leave him for anything because if I did I was always worried about how he was feeling. The second day he got here I remember coming home and packing some clothes to wear for the time I spent at the hospital.

I kept asking the hospital how they would start working on having him talk and walk and they kept saying that they were organizing it but I did not see any signs of them moving around the same to get that going. I used to feel bad for the old man in the other room as he rarely had visitors coming to see him and the way he was hit the other day in our presence I was hoping that he is not treated badly in our absence totally.

The medicines were not given properly to dad. I was completely thorough on what had to be given to him and was monitoring the same. The nebulizers were something that helped him breathe better. That was never given in time. They did not follow the schedule. In fact, the first day they had not given him anything as they said the pharmacy was closed and they had to wait. I told them that if they had informed me I would have gone and gotten it for them.

I met a gentleman who had brought his father for his treatment who was brain dead and the doctors had given up. He was literally here to hand over the parents as they could not keep him home and he was not willing to come back. They looked quite well off and could definitely afford home nursing but looked like they did not care about it and wanted to get rid of the father basically

There was also another daughter like me who was struggling to get some attention from her mother and I could feel her pain as things were not going as per what her doctor had recommended her to do.

There was a main doctor here who looked like he was capable, However the staff in charge at night were like students who were in training and had kept calling the main doctor for consultation. Considering that the patients who came here were critical it was surprising how they did not keep any experienced staff / nurses to attend to people

Dad spent most of the time sleeping or sitting or sitting quietly to himself. Sometimes we engaged in conversation and he used to speak in sign language. Most of the times I used to talk and he used to acknowledge and answer back. But the moments I spent with him here were the most wonderful and also the most painful ones. Wonderful as I got to be with him 24/7 every second which I had never got till now and painful as it was difficult to see someone as strong as my dad- My hero who was so self-dependent and never stretched his hand to anyone till now for help. He used to make the rules, and was always unable to get around. So, seeing him like this, dependent on people even to get up from the bed, was killing me internally.

A week later when I was lying on my portion of the bed I got a call from R and I should say that at that time made me the happiest of all times. He said that seeing how my dad's immunity was keeping him up he was ready to start immunotherapy for him soon. I was super thrilled, He told me it will be expensive and I told him to go ahead with it no matter what the cost was as I was now desperate to do anything to get my dad out of this.

In fact, I had even checked if we could do a lung transplant- However I was informed that lung transplants are not done for cancer cases.

This immunotherapy process would take a couple of days as he will have to apply to a medical governing body. They will need to approve it and then we will get the injection to administer. I asked him to do it as soon as possible. He told me that his secretary will get in touch with me for the paperwork. This call came to me I remember on a Thursday. I was now so happy and went and told my dad about this call and the treatment process which will get him out of this as soon as possible,

He did not seem to react very much. He had gotten into his mind that he was going to die soon and was not very confident of coming out this soon. I was on the moon whatsoever, Dad was always not a very positive person about doctors and medicines and thought he felt the same about this too . I was not going to give up yet . Also, I wanted to get him out of this place soon.

I immediately called R's secretary and she said she will get back to me on what needs to be filled and payment stuff.

That night was the worst night again due to negligence of the hospice. I unfortunately shut my eyes thinking this attender was watching and when I suddenly opened dads reading was around 79 and the oxygen had stopped flowing again. I woke him up and told him to get to the doctor soon. He got the doctor who consulted the main doctor and they gave the Bipap again. This time I had lost it. The main guy came down and I ripped him apart and told him that if his guys had not slept we should not be in this condition.

He started yelling back at me and said he wanted me to take my dad out and I told him that since I am the only one who is wanting her father to survive while everybody just left them at the care here and did not bother. He said that if I went home leaving him here my father would be much better and I was thinking how unimaginable that would have been to leave my dad at the mercy of this place and let them treat him however they wanted. Even with me being here they were so careless. Without me it would definitely be a huge disaster.

I had taken off from work at this time to completely concentrate on my dad. Fortunately for me the project lead who I was working with was an extremely empathetic gentleman and helped me completely during this phase of my struggle. A large part of what I was able to do for my dad was mainly because of the support I got from him.

I did want to get another place and get him out asap as I did not want him to die here. They had now given us a nurse whose first day it was at the job. I got to know she was from some remote village in Tamil Nadu who was being trained how to attend to patients. I was aghast as to how they tried to make it look like a set of professionals but only as a training institute of innocent people. I definitely did not want my dad to be here anymore. But I was not sure what to do and where to go as the treatment was to take some time and the injection to be approved.

Then I made a decision to take him to B and keep him in comfort at least till the time the injection came through and told the doctor that I was doing that. He told me that it will be an expensive affair but I did not want to put dad through anymore of this nonsense at that home. So, I decided to go for it no matter what the cost was . Earlier the doctor had told me that he was finding an option in the hospital wherein they will avoid the daily room rent option and give it at a monthly option . He said he was waiting for some kind of approval for us to go further, I had at this moment told him that till the approvals I will anyway take the room rent option.

From the home I took him to the hospital in the home ambulance. Currently he was just on 1 kg oxygen which was good and helped with a little less stress on his system. This time Rajeev had spoken to the hospital and organized a private ward for him at the cost of a general ward. I will always be grateful to him for doing that .

So, this time when we entered B there was no emergency, I told them it was a regular admission for a treatment later, they took his vitals which they said were not very good. However, it did not need an ICU admission, so we moved him to the general ward which was very spacious. It had two beds and a really neat bathroom. I was glad that dad would now be at peace. There were around eight such rooms but with most critical patients in them. There were two nursing centres but we were catered to from the front desk. This at the moment was a little disappointing as I saw two nurses one of whom was quite hands on and the other one who was not very bothered about what was going on, but whatever the case they seemed much more trained on what needs to be done in in case things go bad and seemed a little more professional than what I had seen so far.

Also, B gave me a good feel as I saw dad improve a lot the last time and he was talking to some extent when he was out of the ICU, the staff at ICU also were kind to him and looked after him like a human being than a patient like how I had seen in many places. I was hoping that this recovery will continue here at during this period also.

Day 1 he settled down but still looked at me for taking him home. He just wanted to get back. While I was handicapped and really wanted to do that I wanted to also ensure that he gets this injection done before I take him home.

During admission at this time this lady fainted and fell down and was kept in the general ward although when checked the statistics were normal. The nurse mentioned that she was just under observation in the regular ward. I went over and she mentioned that she was so depressed and upset over what was happening with dad.

While I wanted to believe what she was saying I actually did not see any of her love and care in action when dad was actually sick. She was more concerned on how to keep the house clean and tidy than actually prioritizing dads health. I do remember one time when I had got him back from the hospital and he had this favourite blanket of his that he used to love using always. Even if he had other blankets this was like a favourite doll of his which gave him comfort when even kept next to him.

After we settled him on the bed he asked for this blanket and I remember he was having this with him when we loaded him onto the ambulance. While I was searching she entered the room and I asked her about the blanket and she said she had washed it and put it out for drying. We had just come home for like 15 minutes and he had not even settled down. Unfortunately, his other thick blanket was already drying and he literally had to use multiple blankets to keep himself warm as the rest of the warm ones we had were heavy. She had done that as apparently it was smelling

I was amazed by her priority of cleanliness versus his comfort. This was not the first time. He used to keep mentioning that this was quite often and I kept pushing it aside asking him to ignore it many times. Now I realized how difficult these things must have made him feel.

He also told me of this incident once when he went to the restroom and none of us were in the house and by mistake the shawl he was wearing, the tip got dirty and he went and slept on the bed with that, she came back home and he told her about it and she got so wild and immediately put the entire bedding to wash leaving him on a cold hard cot.

I still regret thinking I should have taken these things more seriously. He used to say it in such a light-hearted mode that he made it look like it did not affect it at all. But when I was with him and seeing it happen in front of me was very disgusting and I could see how humiliated he was with it. After all that he did and was continuing to do to ensure that all of us were living in comfort .

He used to ask for breakfast at 9 and she was so busy with the net that she used to give it only by 10. A lot of other things were important to her other than caring for my dad especially at the moment he needed it the most

Back at home he used to keep getting up as he was breathless and sometimes had body pain. He used to struggle to sleep at night. Off let he started saying that he kept dreaming of three people digging a grave and that kept resurfacing often. Sometimes he used to get up and say: 'I am scared" I now realized what I should have said is: It's fine to be scared, it's a normal emotion:' ' But I made a mistake by saying "You cannot be scared daddy- You are my hero. I have always been strong seeing how strong you are. If you say that you are scared, then what is the example you are giving me?"

I thought by saying these things he will get stronger. I now realize that I should have let him speak his mind and let him know that if he was scared I was always there for him.

But I am so grateful during the last day when he did mention he was scared I hugged him tight and held him like that for almost an hour and told him that it is fine and he should be ok soon

When they told me, she fainted I did not have any emotions. I really wanted to be with dad. I made her sit in a chair because when I collapsed last time she was with me.

Just to return that favour I stayed with her for about 30 minutes and then went about looking into the admission for dad. He was very sober and did not speak anything,

He asked for my brother and I told him that he had not come. The last time he came to see him was when he was at home almost a week back. I was so hurt that he had made that statement although that is the way he was exactly behaving from the start of when he was diagnosed. Now when I see how things are turning out he actually wanted to ensure that he was ready to get the property very soon.

Once in fact in the hospital dad during a conversation mentioned that he was waiting for him to pass so that he can get the property.

The distance between where he lived and where dad lived was 5 metres in the same compound- He would step in around once in two months to check how he is doing. But he would make it a point to ensure that he came and enquired every time one of his friends came up just to show off to dad's friend that he cared for him. Dad was so smart that he used to always tell me that he would not fall for this drama and knew that he did not care for him at all.

After some time, he gave up asking for him or expecting him to be with him. I think at this point he gave up expecting care from anyone. But I was not going to leave his side no matter what happened . He used to like my elder niece until she took him to the hospital once during my absence. Apparently, she really got hyper and pissed him off so much that when we were at the hospital he actually told me not to trust her anymore. He wanted to give her the bike and given her a duplicate key,

Now in fact he wanted me to tell her that I lost my key and take it from her. I never did it more so that I got busy with his treatment details. He also ensured that he handed over all the property documents over to my hand and told me to take control of the entire proceedings of the house maintenance and look after managing the tenants.

After all this drama we finally got him to the room which looked pretty spacious, and I messaged R thanking him for allowing this for a low cost. We were anyways informed that this will be available only till Diwali as admissions will start post that and we might need to take a separate room thereafter

I had to get him an oximeter from the hospital and I requested them to keep it beside him at all times for me to monitor regularly. I did not want the saturation to drop and then get back to the mode last time when we had to put him on to the Bipap to retrieve his breathing back to normal/

I settled down with my bag and moved my bed which was actually another patient bed as it actually housed two patients and put it next to him so that he does not have to struggle much to get my attention for help

This lady admitted him and went back home and I settled myself in. Although all his statistics were normal he did not look very well. I was never able to figure out what was going on in his mind.

But knowing him for so long I do know that all he wanted was to get back home. Every time he had voiced about going back home I had convinced him saying that I am trying to solve it once for all and then take him home. However, after what he felt at home the last time I got him to the hospital I felt he was better off being here under supervision than at home when no one knew what was happening. I settled him in and then got back to monitoring him as he went to sleep. I did most of the talking telling him how I was trying my best to get him out of this. I did let him know that a new treatment that the doctor thinks will be successful for him. I remember at this time he just shook his head and said that he is expecting to die within three days. I am not sure where he got this idea from but it just tore my heart to see him do this. He was on oxygen at this moment but not on the Bipap. This was quite a good scene for me as I knew that he hated the Bipap. It made him so uncomfortable and even looking at him just hurt. I had tried to convince him how it helps clear the passage and also help him get his speech back but he was not convinced and just did not want this. I remember trying to tell him that even though this is also a painful process for me going through this I am very happy to be there just with him and helping him in this phase. I just wanted him to co-operate in three things — one is to have his food, eat his medicines and try to get some sleep whenever he can. I know for most part of the time he ate just to make me happy. He was at this moment completely out of eating solid food and was on liquids. He never mentioned this again but I kept feeling that maybe he was struggling to swallow food.

I kept asking him every time to ensure that he does not hurt himself but he would keep nodding his head that he did not have any trouble. He however stopped eating all of his favourite foods at this time.

He only started eating things which he did not have to chew much. Another happy news was the fact that I asked the doctor permission to take off the food pipe. He kept saying that was irritating him too and he did not feel like he was eating anything. He could only feel the food in his stomach. He started to have Ensure protein drink and Manna at this time. He never went to the toilet this time for quite a while and I knew he was quite frustrated with this. The doctor kept giving him enema to get his stomach cleaned. One time he pointed to his stomach and said that it was aching due to not going to the toilet. I told the doctor the same and he said that it will settle in quickly.

I tried getting him food that he always liked like noodles and curd rice which he would just have one spoon and then refuse to have. He was happy having Ensure or Manna most of the time. He was having a lot of fruit juices. This time I started getting the hospital food and the food here was much much better compared to what he used to get at the earlier hospital. He was slowly getting weaker by the day. He at this moment even stopped wearing his glasses. He said that he could definitely see better, I was not sure to what extent that was true or not.

He stopped needing his mobile and never asked for it. He kind of lost interest in everything. He was not an Android person how much ever I tried to teach him. He used to love watching the swiggy movement, Map movement on my phone and cutely watched it for hours. I could understand him but only he knew what he was going through. Never someone very vocal about what was happening still to me. I kept thinking that he hopes that he is not putting any burden on me. I was just so hurt seeing him like this but was ready to go to any extent to get him out of this. He kept asking me to get my car and take him home and I just wish today I did that and gave him the comfort of the home – His home at this time.

I was just so desperate to get him out of this. I was shuttling between being with him and even if I went to the restroom he would get nervous and start missing me. I was so careful to leave someone with him before I stepped out and that would be for a maximum time of around 30 minutes either to have something to eat which I would just do once a day mostly because I did not want to leave and also because slowly I was losing my appetite and lost my love for food. I would step out if I got a call for payment also. After coming here, I rarely went home as I had some stuff with me to go on for a few days,

I had also left my workouts, running and meditation which I used to so diligently follow earlier. However, none of this mattered, He was my priority now and I could not move away from him even for a minute. I remember his suddenly waking up one day and asking me if I had gone for my running. Not sure why he suddenly remembered that. I assured him that I will restart all of that after we get back home. Now I was very happy sitting and spending every moment with him.

Even when I stepped out for something my mind will always with him on what he was up to, I could just not take my mind of it, When I went for my bath I would just slightly close the door and keep shouting outside to ensure that he knows I was there,

He would now need a lot of pillows but did not sleep in the night. Most of the time he complained of chest pain and also breathing difficulty.

I was informed on Thursday that I can go ahead with the process of getting the immunotherapy medicine and I got very busy with submitting the papers. There were so many documents to be submitted and I had to put together all his old reports and identity proofs and send them to the person. The person said that only Friday was there as Saturday was closed due to Diwali holidays. Then it would get delayed till Tuesday. I literally begged him to do it asap and I will move anything to ensure that I gave all the documents that he wanted to be provided. He did help me to get approvals verbally and move through the system quicker than expected. The next day again was all about getting paperwork done.

Suddenly dad was now being adamant in eating and even what liquids he was having was being a little difficult. Doctor was saying that if he does not eat then they will have to put on the food pipe soon. The nutritionist also said that they will start giving him some good liquid for a week and try to ensure he gets energized before again removing the pipe. I thought this sounded ok as at least for immunotherapy he needed to get some food down his system.

I knew that he did not like the pipe but something was stopping him from eating and he was not being clear on what that was. The fear was that he would pull off the pipe in the night.

Earlier he did it once and he had also pulled off the urine catheter at night . It must have been so annoying for him to do that because I did get to know that it was an extremely painful process putting this on and much more painful pulling it off. He was never someone who would step into the hospital even for a fever. He would always tell me that you should have your system fight off the disease which will strengthen the immune system and now everything possible from the medical field was being worked upon by him .

On Friday I went home to get some clothes as all my old ones were starting to smell.

Dad always loved to see me in traditional wear rather than the modern stuff. So, from the last two weeks I was ensuring that I only wore traditional dresses around him, not that it mattered much but felt that at least he is not pissed off on that aspect. He would never demand anything but sometimes when we would go out at home he and I were wearing jeans he would very innocently ask – "Are you wearing this' – Also say that don't you have anything else to wear apart from this.

The hospital was almost two hours' drive from him but since I did not have my car and the cab was very expensive I took the metro train and took the auto for the connecting ones. I kept rushing and running as I did not want to miss being with him.

I wanted to ensure that I was always with him and be there for every moment that he wanted me. Maybe I was possessive of him but I loved him to that extent that even a minute away from him was a torture. I literally made it back in about 1 and half an hour, almost double the time this lady used to take going or coming back one way from home and always complaining that she did not get an auto or bus.

She did not like coming to the hospital so far at all but knew she had to do it as a formality. I rushed back to the hospital and set up the bag. He now started liking these twinkies so I got some for him and also gave him some chocolate which he ate. Maybe it was not too much of an effort to swallow which made it easier to eat.

This was a Friday now and the medicines were ready to come in tomorrow to be administered to him.

Once the doctor saw him and asked the nurse to put him back on Bipap. His medicines had come down but had to give him nebuliser and a few medicines along with the CBD oil.

Thursday night he had a very tough night sleeping as he was having breathing problems . I let the doctor know but he said that this is normal and there is nothing that he can give him that might help. I put on some relaxation music to help him but it did not help at all. He just gave me those sad looks of pain and I was so handicapped to do anything at all., I went out and cried and asked God to help him during this time and if possible give me all that pain and take it away from my darling.

I had at this time kept the oxygen meter by his bedside permanently and kept monitoring it regularly, there were no other attachments that were being monitored. His oxygen was quite normal but still they had to give him Bipap for a while now and then and also the nebulizer.

This night again he was having a lot of problems and he had refused to eat. I actually got angry with him and went off to sleep turning my head to the other side, but then I saw him struggling to sit up and had to get up and help him. I forgot the anger and put his head against my shoulder and tried soothing him down but it did not help at all. I also tried on some music but to no avail. I then had to go and call the heart doctor at around 2 in the morning as he was really struggling.

He came and checked up and said nothing was abnormal but then due to his current condition this was expected to happen, I asked them if they could give him some medicines and they wrote him an anxiety tablet which did not help at all.

I told dad that the doctor is saying everything is normal. They asked me if they wanted to do an ECG and dad said no so I said that I will see for one more day and then take a call whether it needs to be done or not,

This moment of him lying on my shoulder and me trying to tell him everything is fine will be something that I will never ever forget in my life. He looked so vulnerable at this moment. One thing I was happy about was that the immune injection was coming in that Saturday and will get him some relief from this mess.

He was a pretty strong man and at that age going through six chemo's and also having been in the ICU three times was not a joke. He was so strong that he was able to take it. I am sure someone at his age would have been very difficult to do that. It was mainly because of his food habits. All the life that I have known him, his food was always strict breakfast at 9 – mainly idly, some rice in the afternoon and some mutton along with cucumber or ragi mudde for the night.

He used to love pickles and I used to get so much for him every time I travelled from Chennai. His morning usually starts off with two raw eggs, sukku coffee, a brisk walk and some breathing all this in the morning by 4.

Till the time he fell sick he used to get up at 2 alternative days to ensure to put on the motor for the tenants so that they did not complain about not having water to drink. He used to have a standard drink every time but only at home, He used to always avoid the drinks when he went out and never a person who would step out for a party or something. The only habit that screwed him up was the smoking, I was hoping at least by the November check-up he could have stopped.

I also sometimes keep thinking if the vaccination had something to make him vulnerable. But I guess this is how the human brain is. If he passed away and I had not vaccinated him maybe I would think about this happening because I did not vaccinate him.

So, seeing such a strong person lying on my shoulder literally made my heart bleed for him. My hope was just that neither day nor treatment would start.

Next day was Saturday. As he kept complaining about his legs getting numb I brought him some kind of socks that would help blood circulation. I put it around his now skinny legs and hoped it would be able to curb this discomfort.

I went to take my bath and told him that I will be out very soon. He was again in that sad mood more so because of the pain he was going through, I stepped out again and from the crack of the door told him that I will not be long. I was not even concentrating on my bath. I just wanted to finish very soon and get back to him. The day before also the same happened. The entire hospital was in a festive mood for Diwali which was on Sunday. In fact, when I went to talk to Rajeev to request him to sign off the mail that the immune guy had sent he was distributing sweets to all and the staff were given a special lunch. Here all the nurses I would say were good, but they just did what was instructed to him and like I have been seeing for all along and talking through here I see very less of that passion and compassion, they just looked at my dad as someone who was a commodity. I was not sure if it was his age and priority was for younger people. However, if that was the case then it saddens me more as we cannot neglect old people and let them die, they also need care and maybe much more so that they do not feel neglected even if they going through a critical phase and they are made to feel loved and wanted, I felt that lack completely in all the hospitals I visited

In Philomena's once when the doctor in front of the nurses said that he was critical and a night after two days I went to ask the nurse if I could remove the BiPap. She was so abrupt about it and I told her to be gentle. She in front of my dad says- Mam you know what the doctor said right, He does not have much time" I had to take her outside and tell her to be sensitive to what my dad can hear.

In fact, I sometimes wondered what these doctors and trainees have spoken in from of my dad to make him feel hurt or make him lose hope, He was always hopeful that he would come out of this very soon, I would never know if some conversations of these people somehow gave him that feel that something was really wrong and he was not going to get well at all.

In the morning he had a juice of musk melon and after sometime I asked him if he wanted to have Ensure for which he said yes. I was so glad he was eating this time. I had also made a promise to myself that I will never get angry with him no matter what happens. The guy was also called to put back the tube as he started making a fuss to eat lunch which was also a favourite of his – Curd rice,

I realized that he only ate what I gave him. This lady had got something to eat and he refused to eat.

She came in surprisingly early and was there by 12. The nurses went about doing their work – Some of them I felt did not have much maturity by the basis of how they spoke and interacted with me. While many of them were really kind and sweet they showed the fact that they had just stepped out of college and were still in the training phase. It was around 1:30 that they called me in the billing department and I had stepped out for asking them what they wanted,

I specifically told this lady to keep an eye on the oxygen meter and went out, after clarifying I came back and noticed that the reading was around 79 and it kept dropping, I also noticed that the oxygen was taken off and screamed at what was happening and they said they were transitioning between the nebulizer and the oxygen mask. I screamed at the nurse to put back the oxygen and get him on the BiPap really quickly. While I was desperately doing this, I asked them to call the duty doctor. They did not pay much attention to the urgency and dad was just gasping for breath. This scene is something that I will never forget in my life either. This has happened before but we have got him up with the BiPap and we tried to do that again. It did not help. Slowly it started to go to around 45 and I was yelling for the duty doctor. I also urgently called Rajeev and he said he will come and have a look. But no one moved at the speed I wanted them to move. I was holding his hands and telling him to breathe in and that he could do it. I realized that maybe the Bipap was making him even more uncomfortable and asked them to remove that so that he can naturally start getting the oxygen back again. While I keep saying I did it- it was definitely all against the doctors checking,

The duty doctor came and felt his pulse and said that there are no chances of him surviving. I picked up the rosemary that my sister Celine had given me along with the Ganesh idol I kept near his bed and gave it to which he clutched really strongly. I was just praying that he would come back . I was informed that the immune medicine had already reached the hospital and I was sure that once he survived this then I can get him back on to good life conditions.

I went to the nurse stations and was actually shocked to see the indifference at a lot of them. I yelled at them on why did they not give the oxygen and even at this lady that I had to just step out for like thirty minutes and she did not have the common sense to check the meter, this is the reason why I would always want to be sitting next to him as even other instances even at home and I have noticed her busy with the phone and not noting the reading or talking unnecessary stuff with the nurses and losing track of why she was here

Once Dad had pooped and I had sent her outside to get a nurse and a man to come and help clean-up and get him up on the bed. After about 5 minutes I went out and saw her chatting stories with someone in the kitchen. I asked her why she did not get the person and then she will always have some kind of a story to tell no matter what the situation is. This time she was chatting with the nurse when I walked in to see the drop so much. Dad was grasping and tears were falling out of eyes so much.

The doctor had still not come. I did not have my shoes and I ran down to his room. He was with a patient, I begged him to come and see dad and he came along with me to the top floor. He looked at my dad and asked both of us to come with him. He took us to a separate room and made us sit there,

Now at this stage a lot of nurses have come into the room and even his secretary had walked in along with the psychiatrist and they were saying that the way to was encouraging was the best anyone could do- I kept telling him that I love him so much and he is so strong that he is come out of so many things that this was nothing and I wanted him to fight for me as he could not leave me an orphan and go.

In the room Rajeev told us that it was time to let him go and the best thing to do was to go to his ear and say god's name. I did not want to let him go like this; this was very painful. I was not ready to lose him as yet.

I went back to him and kept requesting him to be strong and pull him the breadth as he usually does. He kept doing it but I knew he was struggling.

I went out for a minute and prayed that let all that pain be transferred to me and take me instead of him. I realized that I cannot let him struggle like this and had to do something. I then decided to take him to the ICU   , something Rajeev had totally requested me not to do. I wanted to give him a chance as I knew if I get him off now it will be best to put him for further treatment. I called Rajeev and he was not very happy doing this but then they organized a stretcher and moved him to ICU.

He was still gasping for breath when they moved him inside and after an hour of waiting in the lobby. This was the most painful moment of my life and time almost came to a standstill.

The doctor called me and asked me to come to the ICU. I went up and she told me that he is critical. They tried to get him on the Ventilator but he is still struggling to breathe. They said that it is very difficult for him to make it. His heart apparently beat to around 30 and started to increase but then started dropping again. However, they had mentioned it to me almost three times and I was hoping that this time also it did not turn out to be the truth. I went down and waited for some more information. They called me again at around 5:45 and asked me to come on top. I ran up and went to the ICU. I saw this doctor at the door who was the duty doctor and asked him if I had come to see my dad Thevar. What really struck me and this will never ever go out of my life forever and also the fact that I want to talk to this gentleman when I do meet him shows that empathy is not his game.

As I went running and mentioned dads name his response was who? And I said Thevar and he just said "oh he is no more" – I was shocked and my brain did not know what to register. They had moved him to the right side of the room to help recover him as against all the other people who were being kept to the left. I could not walk. I felt I tried but the floor was being moved away but then rushed to the room and then followed by my brother.

I looked at him on the bed with a pipe in his mouth. In the gown that he was wearing for so many days. Lifeless- I could not believe it. He was no more- He would not call me "Sundhari" He would not ask me to come to Bangalore anymore. He would not ask to order chicken biryani anymore and would not call me to recharge his mobile anymore: He was no more- I hugged him close and asked him to get up. Begged him to get him to get up. He did not just listen.

I knew this was the end. With him he took the life from me also. He took the basic essence of my existence with me. However, I felt he was free from this pain he was suffering. Maybe he tried fighting for me to come back and be with me for some more time but then gave up as it was too much to bear. Maybe his heart beat for me too . This is all I could think of when I was looking at his face.

There was this tube into his mouth I guess which they had inserted when trying to revive him. I called Rajeev and told him he was gone. He told me to be brave and strong. My strength just died. My life just died, I did not know what was there left in me anymore. They told me to step out while they brought him outside. I stepped out and my friend had come in along with her husband. I was so glad they were there as my brother and dad's second wife had ganged up as usual and were couped up in one corner, I wanted to be far away from them. Seething in anger that he was not there for dad even at his last breath , He came and held on to me and I told him to leave me alone which hurt his mighty ego.

He screamed and went around to do the formalities. They gave me a form to sign to take him out of the hospital. Till now I have signed a lot of forms for him including his gun license application, his property tax papers and also his deposit receipts. This was not something I wanted to sign and I refused to do it.

My friends told me that this is the least respect I can show for my dad and get this done for him. After all I had to do this as this was something that I deserved doing than anyone else. I signed all the paper and then requested them to kindly hand over his gown that he was wearing which they refused. I literally begged them and asked the doctors to please help me here and finally they gave me his gown. They told me that the better option is to keep him in the morgue today and then take him over for the morning and I refused to listen to that, I knew how he felt when he was very cold and it scared me to have him left all alone here while I stayed out as I was definitely not planning to go back home without him. My brother asked me to pay for the ambulance while my friend told him to at least to get that done and they organized to him taken home. Now my brother was very keen to finish all formalities at this moment and everything worked at clock work. He had set up the shamiana and all that. It was as if like he was waiting for him to pass away like how my dad used to always keep saying. I remembered again for the 10th time. If he had shown so much concern when dad was alive maybe we could have made it more comfortable for him for a while at least.

I laid my dad on dads chest all the way back home and almost could feel his heart beating or maybe that's what I wanted to happen. One good thing though was that there were absolutely no traces of any of the tube, food pipe or any other marks on his face at all. There was a mark on his nose where they had kept the BiPap and it had all got dried and was black. Now however even that was not visible and he looked so happy in his sleep. This was at least making me feel a little glad. Maybe he was telling me that he was fine. Maybe he was telling me that he had escaped all the pain that he was suffering. However, I was still hoping somehow, he would get up and the doctors would say they made a mistake and he was fine. That did not happen . We laid him down at home -His home that he built with so much difficulty and brother washed him down. I felt the chi illness when his body was getting washed down. He had refused both due to the chillness . This lady used to pour cold water down his body and was never sensitive to wiping it down fast as he would be shivering in the cold.

He was all decked up as per the customs and they were about to close the ice box over him which I did not allow to happen. I still did not want him to feel the severe chillness on his body. He had already felt a lot of cold at many instances. I still kept looking at him to open his eyes and did feel that his eyes were opening up slowly. They agreed to leave the cover open so that I could hug him the whole night and that's exactly what I did.

I slept with my head on his chest. I could not sleep as I was still scared that he would harm himself as he used to when he was alive out of anger. But I think due to the tiredness I automatically fell asleep. Before going to sleep I prayed to dad and told him that if you really loved and forgave me for being impatient sometimes which was purely to get him back to health than give me some signals that he will always be with me and will always love me. I really could not have made this up but I felt his heart beat three times. I immediately looked up but there was absolutely no change on his face and I still again felt if there was a mistake the doctors made in declaring him dead. I could not believe this was happening. After I fell asleep I could see it drowning into quick sand completely. This was being displayed on what I used to see in the hospital monitors. He was going down slowly and there was nothing I could do to save him . I wanted to jump in with him but somehow just could not reach the quick sand place. I could literally see his face till the eyes completely covered up and then suddenly he comes out of it and he wipes his face. The sand is not pulling him down anymore and he is smiling. He tells me that he can now breathe and is perfectly fine, I just got up with a gasp and then realized I was dreaming but however what happened in the next 2 minutes is something that I am not able to explain till now. There was this sudden wisp of light/Air I could not fathom that went from his body to mine and it startled my body for a while. It was a beautiful feeling though, I looked around. Everybody was sleeping in their rooms and I was all alone with dad. I was hoping he saw how much I loved him and still forgave me for being impatient with him sometimes.

This however left me feeling very good and I went back and laid on his chest to see if he could give me any more messages. Morning dawned, and I did not want to wash or freshen up. I just wanted to lie with him and never get up and just go with him where he was being taken to. My life without him was useless. I did not want to live a life like that anymore. I wanted him back. Friends started coming in to see him. Everybody came and spoke so well of him and all the help that he had done. Many were shocked on how such a strong man vanished suddenly and especially after he was pulling through the disease and everybody thought he would make it through, I was at this moment to myself and the lawyer uncle was the only one who was my strength of support at this moment, I was so glad he was. Maybe my dad planned it in such a way for him to be there, He had apparently taken a promise from him to stay with me and help me out throughout. I was glad some of my friends came to give me the strength and support that I very much needed at this moment, it was as if someone just took the floor away from the ground and I was left hanging in mid-air gasping for breath and fresh air which was possible only to be given by my dad.

After everyone left it was now time to move him to the last rites to the crematorium. They were looking for his Aadhar card. He had handed over all his papers to me and I had not even looked at him and I did know it was in there. When I looked later I found it and gave it to them. They got him over to the van and we drove down all the way to the crematorium. I looked around on the way and saw these were the roads both of us had roamed around on his bike., So we both used to take off on his vehicle and just go off roaming and have some coffee in some nice shop and sit and gossip about stuff. We had so many stories to tell each other, Now then looking at these roads tore at my heart and every single memory kept popping up now and then. I wanted to come to these places again but with him alive. We used to visit each of these banks and have a good chat with all the people and everyone in the bank used to love him and treat him so well except for Vijaya bank where there was absolutely no customer empathy at all. This bank I used to hate to go and hence dad used to never make me go here most of the time. I had opened up accounts in two banks and he managed all the accounts of mine from here. He was in control of both and he ensured I didn't withdraw money from both and kept saving for mine own good... I used to give all my check books to him to manage. I remember one time when his friend wanted money and he asked me to lend him 10 lakhs. I told him to please take as much as possible and handle it. That was how we managed each other's money, I never used to think twice if it came to spending for him and he used to also feel the same. We discussed financial stuff together very freely . He knew exactly what was happening with my money and I knew where he had his.

I have to mention that when I went back to this same friend for some money at the last stage he refused to lend me any.

I used to buy for him freely and somehow the price tag was something I never looked at when it came to him. It was a moment of total happiness when he would just call me and ask me to order something on Swiggy for him. These were very rare moments that he would ask me anything, He was always someone that would not ask anybody anything especially me. But for things that I used to buy for him for example his liquor, some utensils, household stuff he used to ask me to keep an account and then pay me a lump sum amount

The last time when about three months back there was total of 60000 and he insisted on paying me back., I told him it can wait till he is fine and he refused to listen so I allowed him to deposit the cheque which unfortunately came back due to the wrong year, He was in such an urgency to give me another cheque to clear it up. When I asked him, what was the hurry he used to be like when I die I don't want to die as someone who owed money to people.

Even at some point he wanted to know how much I had spent for him as he wanted to write it off. I had always told him not to worry about that part of the account as it was my responsibility to manage that part, I told him that I will ensure that I will manage that some way or the other and he should not bother himself on that.

All of these memories came crashing to me as we headed towards the crematorium and there he lied – all his 76 years before him. It made me realize one thing at that time. He made property, slogged it out- Not enjoyed a lot for him – I used to keep telling him to spend it on him as much as possible but he used to refuse to do that, Now I realized that he actually saved it for me and also insisted on cheaper hospitals options as he did not want the money to run out for me. I realized that he did not take anything with him when he was going into the chamber.

All that he took with him was these words of all those hundreds of people who came to send him off and how kind he was and how much he used to help people with his kindness- He never pinched for money and he would freely ensure that he does not borrow any money from people and actually he did not. He in fact would lend to people and keep an account diligently of it.

This was human life . At the end of it, the only thing that mattered was what you did to people to help them. Not how much money you had. And he had done a lot for the people. That was why there was so much crowd at his funeral. I Kept staring at him. My brother did the last rites but I wanted to take part in everything he did and actually went against the rules to do what only the son does.

I did not know how this mattered, but I knew that this would have made my dad very happy as he always wanted me to be with him always and I did not want to step out at this time of need.

Somehow with my determination even the Guruji did not make a big noise and allowed me to perform all the rights equally. Everyone broke down the hardest when they sent him towards the chamber, they screamed and cried and even I thought I would do the same. Having someone with you from the time you are a baby and then suddenly seeing them turned to ashes was unfathomable and I really thought that I might just break down. Surprisingly I suddenly felt this strange invisible hand holding me and whispering to me " It's just a body" I will always be with you, I know I could never have imagined that as not a drop of tear came from my eyes. In fact, I found this profound strength which made me stand up straight and look at his body being going into the chamber. I did not feel anything at all except love for this strong presence next to me. These are somethings I am not unable to explain as they are not normal but I can only sense these and glad for these moments totally as they made me feel that he is still around somewhere helping me and loving me as much as I love him.

It was all done in about one minute and they told us we could collect the ashes the next day,

A strange sense of emptiness. A loss of battle for me, I tried to save him. But I could still feel that hand holding me tightly. I think he realized this might be the time I might collapse and went against all odds to ensure that he let me know that he was there with me.

We went back home and I went upstairs where he had specifically built this place for me and never rented it out even when I was not staying there. He made it my design wish and   I stayed there always when I came to Bangalore. This time I stayed without him downstairs. I had never done this at all.

I have never stayed in that house without him. He was always there when I was there. Whenever   I was in Bangalore he used to wait for me till 9 in the morning as that was the time I would step down to have breakfast with him. He would wait till I came down and then u would sit with him and work on my laptop and step into the first room when I had calls. Sometimes I had so many calls that he would hesitate so much to come over and talk to me. Initially I used to tell him that I will finish the call and come, however in September 2021 I lost my dog to old age. He used to love going for walks and when I was not working I used to take him for long walks. After I got the job I stopped taking him out and he used to keep coming and barking at me . I used to tell him that I have work and cannot take him out. When he was unable to walk and was almost at the stage of putting him to sleep while my dad kept him up till I came back from my trek I took up his leash and begged him to get up for a walk and he could not. That's when I realized how important it is to take that time to spend with people who mattered to you the most. Also, I remember I was asked to get onto this call when I informed the team that my dog is lying in the backyard about to breathe his last.

So, whenever he came into the room to speak I ensured that whatever I was doing I would put it on hold and ask him what I needed. He was my priority. Only thing I feel is that I could have done this to a larger extent than what I did. Maybe I just quit my job and completely spent the rest of his time with him and I knew that is what he wanted. I was worried about the money for sure and how I was going to manage the same for the medical expenses. Insurance was something that got messed up and never got sorted even till the time he was about to depart.

It felt strange not sitting there with no one waiting for me to come down to eat with him. I did not want to stay in this place any longer. Every turn of my head reminded me of him and it was just so painful. I so wanted to head back to Chennai. However, there was a custom of submerging his ashes in the sea. We had selected Srirangpatna and that was to happen on the third day. Fortunately, due to some start changes we were asked to do it the next day itself. This was a blessing as I could do that and move to Chennai in the same train from there and that's exactly what I did.

In Chennai, as I entered the house, the house which I only selected thinking that I will get him to stay here luxuriously now felt so empty, all those decorations a waste. I was still angry with God and upset that the only wish I asked him was to keep my dad happy and healthy and that is what he did not do. As I opened the door a friend called me to be online till I settled down. I walked into the hall which was very dark. I moved on to switch on the light and on my right saw the pooja room and mentioned to my friend that I am going to remove all the God photos from there and just keep dads and moms photos as they were at least living proof of love. I just turn around and at the extreme corner of the room of the hall were there Christmas lights attached to battery installed and I was shell shocked to see them twinkling, I had not even gone close to them and they run on batteries which if left on even by mistake will not last for more than two days maximum but I have not stepped into this house for the last two months. There was a little flutter in my heart – was dad indicating that he was with me. I then crashed down and slept for all those months I missed sleeping and woke up with this severe back pain. Then the body started giving up. Till now I had an objective to fight for. A motive to look forward to saving dad, now nothing and my body started to give up. I went to the other bedroom which I specifically set up for my dad when he might visit Chennai and he had never come to this house although he has visited the others. He actually liked coming here for short breaks sometimes and I had set up the place specifically for him. Another shock awaited me. The

AC was on and I have not switched on that AC for almost the time I had just fixed it. It had a standalone switch away from the normal switch box and I could not fathom how even by mistake I could have switched it on. This however were giving me spurts of hope that he was definitely there somehow and I sent him a quiet prayer to keep communicating with me,

After that I kept seeing lights on and off randomly and still see them. I wrote to Physics and mediums to have them talk to him and come back with a message for me. Some means to show me that he is still with me and it's just in another world and in a matter of time I would also be with him.

As the legal stuff was being handled I saw the actual side of my family on how greedy they were to get their hands on the property, They still not get it that like dad no one takes anything with them when they go, There was no point fighting like this over this land, I was clear that I did not want it to give benefit to anyone that did not treat my dad well or to whomsoever he did not want it to be given to. I was even willing to hand it over in charity but definitely not to these scavengers.

I had both his numbers and phone with me. He wanted it to be with me. He used this simple button phone and was very happy with it . He used to look so cute trying to make a call by typing one key after another. In many ways I found a lot of innocence in my dad. He had no clue on how this world had changed.

He had given me the key to his cupboard. He had two keys. One he had given me a few years back when he visited Chennai and now one. I had never opened his cupboard. But by the time I came to Bangalore again this lady had broken open his cupboard and all the money and jewellery he said was there was missing. I left it at that .

Conclusion

Many tell me that time will change things. It will get better as the days pass by. It doesn't . The pain gets worse. I miss him more and feel unbelievable as the days pass that he is not with me anymore. But I only mean physically. I can feel his presence otherwise in all that I undertake to do. I see his blessings on how things get smoothly closed.

I feel his presence when I make some decisions and it works for the best. He makes me know in many ways that he loves me a lot and will never leave my side no matter how long it takes.

He was the most understanding and the cutest dad any daughter can ask for. He never spoke of his love much. He did not have to. His actions spoke volumes about what he felt for me. The conversations in the hospital are all I need for my lifetime. Those were priceless. We spoke about everything and everyone. He made me understand that nothing apart from me mattered to him in this world. He said that he would not spend much even when I had asked him to earlier as he wanted to save it all for me. For my future and my security.

I now wait to finish my work that I intended to do here and meet him again on the other side.

I want to thank my friends Femina, Tara, Sameena, Vani, NG Rajesh, Aruna and Pooja, Chelvi, Ramesh, Shankar, Samrat, Kumar, and many more .

Special thanks to my Dad's friend Jayachandran and Vasudevan

Another person who stood by me and a mere "Thank you" will not hold good is Kalpana, Arvind and Ranjith. I could not have done it through so far without you guys

The message I personally learnt from this journey is that please take your decisions carefully, be patient when they get diagnosed and explore all options on treatments and hospitals carefully before settling down on something.

Do your research and do not blindly go by these searches that you will find on the net.

It's a painful journey.

I want to thank my friends Femina, Tara, Sameena, Vani, NG Rajesh, Aruna and Pooja, Chelvi, Ramesh, Shankar, Samrat, Kumar and many more.

Special thanks to my Dad's friend Jayachandran and Vasudevan

Another person who stood by me and a mere "Thank you "will not hold good is Kalpana, Arvind and Ranjith.I could not have done it through so far without you guys